<u>*All Love Frequency ~ In Zero Space*</u>

Sunny Jetsun

All Love Frequency ~ In Zero Space

Sunny Jetsun

Books by the Same Author:

'Driving My Scooter through the Asteroid Field
Coming Down Over Venus ~ Hallo Baba'
'Light love Angels from Heaven. New Generation,
Inspiration, Revolution, Revelation ~
All the Colours of Cosmic Rainbows'
*'Green Eve * Don't lose the Light Vortex **
My brain's gone on holiday ~ free flowing feelings'
'Surfing or Suffering ~ together * Sense Consciousness
fields of a body with streams and stars of hearts'
"When You're happy you got wings on your back ~
Reposez vos oreilles a Goa; We're only one kiss away"
Psychic Psychedelic
'Streaming Lemon Topaz Sunbeams'
'Invasion of Beauty *FLASH* The Love Mudras'
*Patchouli Showers * Tantric Temples*
'It's Just a Story ~ We Are All the Sun, Sweet Surrender'
Anthology #1 ~ 'Enjoy The Revolution'
Anthology # 2 ~ 'Love & Freedom ~ Welcome'
'He Lives In a Parallel Universe'
'Queen of Space ~ King of Flower Power ~ dripping Rainbows'
*Peace Goddess*Spirit of the Field*The Intimacy Sutras*
'Heavenly Bodies ~ Celestial Alignments*
Feeling ~ Energy that Is LOVE in Itself'
'I've been to Venus & back*These Are Real Feelings*
Let the Universe Guide Your Heart*through Space'
* The Kiss in Slaughterhouse 6 *

This book is arranged from 'Surreal' notes made from Inspired
conversations with friends during the 2012/2013 winter season
in Anjuna, Goa ~ Thank You * Happy Days * Om Shanti Shanti

Life is simple ~
Sharing Loving Kindness
from the heart

Padma's Fragrances

My light soul received you as a tsunami of delicious Tantric Bliss.
I'll see your Love reflecting in the skies ~ in your eyes above me.
Very soon I'll be waiting in Euphoria as a lustful Satyr for the Passion
train to arrive bringing you into my arms, a sexy, gorgeous nymph
in her long socks & tutu covering a delirious, sweet arse to die for!
We're flying in that direction ~ Playing in fountains of ecstasy,
brilliantly lighting up a space for you to come to me in intimacy.
I'm sending you Solar flares of Love through the grey sky to
stoke your heart, filling it with temptation & Fucking DESIRE.
I also know about being in a stagnant place and going Crazy
in this Matrix of Insanity. I'm so happy that tomorrow we will be
*together * Enlightened with the stars in our PERFECT harmony*

*

Seeing through clouds

"This World seems to be run by unscrupulous criminal gangs!"
'Fear' the Idea that we are separate ~ 'Dividing & Conquering'
Head adjusting your perceptions of reality ~ Can you see Infra-
Red spectrums, gamma rays, touch wifi; feel Invisible O Zone bliss?
Got a letter from the Universe ~ What is your job on Earth?
Wanna keep 'em poor in Absolute slavery; Protecting your Property!
"I've got that many things in my life I've got no reason to be unhappy"
We must always speak the truth ~ That should be on billboards,
like night moving in the empty streets, the grass growing on the hill.
"Seeing the King & Queen naked, you get to see it's all bollocks!"
'Unite' ~ Honorary Citizens of the Republic of Money & Greed.
Found a Peace Loving Emperor ~ living in an Asylum!
Ask Richard Dadd of 'the fairy fellers master stroke'....
Fruit trees giving you its fruit freely. "How good is that!"
'Ignorance is Bliss' ~ I'll take the bliss,
you can have the Ignorance if you want

1

Goa Work-Out!
They have to let go of their emotions ~ allowed to make a Holi mess!
Let All Colours Be ~ Breaking the light, no judgment, doesn't matter.
"Do you prefer blue ocean, black sky, aqua marine, red sunbeam?"
"If you Concentrate on a Point you can contact the essence"
"I'm Drop Out Baba" & "I'm Human Space*Ship Baba"
Hip Yoga, India is a big lesson in 'No Expectation'
'Seeing the Relationship Is Just Relating'
Grid Lock! ~ Old Ideas put in New context.
"Feeding myself with mangoes like Crazy!"
In the Multi ~ dimensional Garden of Eden

*

Gurus are like a SHANTI Signpost
"Be still and know that I AM * God." That simple I AM ~ Is the being.
Satguru ~ None of that: 'not as good as you or I am better than you.'
No gurus, no leaders, no teachers, no Oligarchs, no Holy Emperors!
Don't need all the things just to be; Right to no violence, life in Peace

*

Bacchus' Vice Squad
Looking at life in a sumptuous, new visionary, miraculous way.
Only had an ordinary construction of the Mind ~ Now inspiration!
Add some surreal imagination, dreaming of angels and geishas.
Perfumed genitalia* her love seed ~ blossoming voluptuousness.
Bursting buds of an opening lily ~ no evil in this divine beauty.
Pursuing a delicious dijn out of a tantric jar across a polar star.
The arts of gallantry satisfying all our passions ~ full intercourse.
Super Moksha offering release from further transmigration ~
not becoming any Slave of desires but loving her lustfulness,
delirious, gorgeous glamour, assisted by pure mind & spirit.
Sharing our frolicking organs of sacred sensuality

Imbued with Love

"Understand how Cruel people are by nature!" Stony faced…
All got a cross in their gardens but they'll all piss in front of it.
Conversion > "There's only One coming down and it's Love!"
'A gang rape in Delhi on a moving bus in broad daylight'
The Capital of India ~ made into a joke of Law & Order!
Stripped naked, dumped on the road; stupid, evil men did that.
Another Date rape, with these pills she'll never remember!
No problem you can buy them down at the local Pharmacy!
Yet they won't let her have a cell phone in Orissa denying
her own protection; There's predatory beasts all over!
Haryana girls burnt by their in-laws for their dowry!
Violated girls in Punjab legally made to marry their Rapist!
'Freedom for a woman to be safe and to be herself now!'

*

Confession ~ Compassion

The Party at the end of time ~ still a little hippy at heart.
"I am a good girl ~ wanna be a bad girl in wild Chapora"
He was hallucinating Hanuman ~ Which Reality Is Real?
MDMA pancakes, Acid rocking horses, One big chill Pill!
"But Red Riding Hood killed the wolf, in the fairy story!"
Making furniture you can carry with you in one hand;
Going to the top of a mountain. Living to EXCESS ~
Five senses trembling on the Plateau. He can feel the beat.
She Is An Archangel ~ I fell in Love with a beautiful deaf girl
With a Cocaine Monster, the demon was a fucking badger!
"Come I've got you, You can't say No to me." Powder Face.
Heavy Masks dripping with iridescent diamonds.
What more do you want ~ never satisfied!
Victims of a 'Head on a stick' energy ~
or too relaxed falling out the hammock!

3

Organ's Spasms on Shiva's Moon
Living in delusions and then I just lit up!
"One of those experiences you'll never forget"
Wrote a book of love poems, living in Benares.
'Let's have sensual pleasures not the Apocalypse'
Who lived deliciously with her ~ Perfect Asstrology.
Manipulating her Yoni, teased it open like a flower.
Singing from her heart ~ reconnecting with his muse.
She had no sense of sin, shame, just a free, natural fuck.
'The Rule of Reason is 'Control' ~ to Magical Imagination'
'Following our desires to the absolute limits, gently, lovingly'
*

'Girandola'
A revolving wheel from which rockets were fired.
For some pedophile twat; Where's the Pope when you need one?
You don't wanna sleep in fear at night. All these requirements,
back straight, head up ~ Lotus position or can't get to Nirvana.
What happens you got chronic arthritis? Not Feeling very wavy.
"Why did you surrender to Fear?" Condemned to be a SLAVE!
Visionary context ~ Helen of Troy abducted for her fatal beauty.
Someone started a War! Did you rob them of their divine lives?

"Your dreams cannot become True unless You wake up"
History recording the Official Version; They're trained in it.
Some are still living the holocaust and we're standing back!
"One day all this murder will have to be made accountable"
'We believed in it completely, I was just moving up the ladder'
We will realize what we don't want to live anymore.
And that brings us all together in possible Peace ~
The flame is changing ~ Gold, violet, platinum, purple appearing.
More truth from the cleansing, transmuting ~ Crystal light in you.
*Culture of fear making people do barbaric things! **I am free spirit***

Navel Impetuosity

The mounting of an ass, congress of a cow, jumping Tigers!
Breasts exposed, rubbing, holding, clasping, pressing close.
Generating love, friendship respect in the hearts of women,
shouting, screaming at that moment of Cosmic carnal orgasm!
Wild flowers hanging from her loose flowing hair in full disarray.
Her willingness to act the man's part, sitting on top of his tongue,
breathing hard ~ signs of her wanting enjoyment and satisfaction.
Overpowered by Kisses, by licking ~ sucking deep, his erect penis.
Touching with his hands her thrusting body ~ pulling him into her.
Fingers delving in between her thighs, raising hips, bighting lips.
Unhurried sex while riding on the back of an elephant

*

Lingham Form ^Yoni Yoga

Accomplishes Venus' object using roots, bulbs and erotic fruit.
Balmy, rich unguents, Kama practiced with virgins of all castes.
Obedient tender beginnings rot force, oozing from her heavenly slit.
Sent her to sacrifices, teaching the parrots to speak after breakfast.
Stroking her smoking hips affording us the greatest mutual pleasure.
Imagination in Lovemaking ~
perfuming her luscious, dusky labian pink lips.
Awaiting succulence, magnetism of joy, as long as our mouths kiss.
The current of her sexuality ~ sensuality is too strong to resist!
'Looking into her body not out from it'
Asking her for a full Love Massage…

*

Full Druggie!

"You don't go anywhere on Coke ~ Your Ego does"
The worst trip, it can be used and Abused. Be True to Yourself!
Prison of your own Mind, keeps us trapped here in birth & death.
"The line gets bigger and fatter ~ coming back for an overdose!"

5

Perfect * Pleasurette

'Fondling hard a woman accustomed to stand in doorways
and to stare at passersby ~ A woman steeped in seduction.'
Delicious, lascivious, libidinous, lusciousness, stroking languor.
Belly to belly ~ mouth to mouth, the mutually adorable shocks!
He'll always love you ~ feeling the intensity of her vulva's heat.
Pounding the spot, activating the enjoyment of her maidenhead.
Enflaming her passions, quenching all of her voracious desires.
Seizing a crack in the wall devoid of flesh, raising up her knees
penetrating into some unusual places ~ 52 types of active Yoni.
Rati's unrestrained lustful voluptuousness, ascending MY throne

*

Yearning Suckers

'May God grant us the use of such a vulva' ~ "Amen"
Special exertion, ardour increasing simply at its memory.
Kisses her neck, hair, coaxing her to perform carnal copulation
thrusting her tongue into his mouth. Met a Cosmic Fuck Chick.
Impressions of his biting on her lower lip; Enjoying the woman.
She is your field, enter, plough her as you will, mount upon this.
Constricting tight her Yoni holding your lingham tighter and longer!
Moving her waist back & forth, up & down, churning gyrations.
Here eating your pussy ~ fell into her Venus' honey trap.
'Juiciness impossible to resist her'

*

We only get better ~ Creating is Intent

Learning over it ~ Diamonds sparkling from the pressure.
Spiraling up the Mind ~ Shakti, feminine in the light structure.
Multiple facets with the light creating your 5th dimensional beauty.
Let's get you one of those grass skirts ~ in fields of free hemp dew.
Elephants eating it up; Every question is stupid, you are the Answer!

6

'El Purgatorio'

"Do mosquitoes live in Mosques?" Which f.... sad racist said that?
'Shot her in the face on the school bus, said this 14 year old was
promoting western education values; Where's your values from?'
What a bunch of bloody maniacs, stealing all the bodies at dawn.
Swimming in rivers of corpses ~ diving through hell's melting flames.
Seems unfathomable to destroy ~ Fire's purifying Negative Forces!
Dangerous, Powerful energies; All around but couldn't see it.
There's the Prince of the Apocalyptic Night.
I need a Cosmic healing right now!

*

Pachamama Dhamma

Original muse ~ creative partnering with a gorgeous arse.
Delicious Surrealist with bliss burning in your shining eyes.
This is the Cosmic Ocean ~ penetrating you in perfect pleasure.
Labia vibrating in the warm breeze of desire, exalted in paradise
This is heaven ~ loving you, being loved by you in deep passion.
Sultry, sublime, lascivious, languid, telepathic dreaming
of your moist Pink Universe, wet as a rainforest inside.
Poses her luscious femininity ~ sex on her sensual mind.
Let's have some raunchy primordial coition in flagrante ~
Bye bye resemblance to beauty, different vision of reality.
Going beyond the limits ~ stripping her down to the core

*

Swinging Pendulums ~ Hemispheres of Sensation

These Images are here to make you realize ~ evoking our Humanity…
The wrong psychological concept ~ who'll appreciate her HEART Art?
What you got to lose and everything to gain by opening up to creation!
Grow your 'Wa' watching the Sunrise and set in a Rothko Mindscape.
Reaction to this bloody massacre, satisfaction of this bloody birthright!
Do you want to take a sedative or enjoy a moment of blissful ecstasy?

Fluffy Ville
I didn't believe any of it but I wanted a coat of many colours.
Go in the free spirit and find a clear pool to reflect yourself in.
Even hugging a tart for free is an experience. Forget Normal!
The trance of not well adjusted children ~ lots of identity issues;
took them to an underground squat, techno party. I like Expansive!
She said she loved the Sociopath and Adolph was a vegetarian!
Give them the Avocado drops ~ swallowing Vitamin D forever.
Getting a Stair Master to my car! Do some 'Very Easy Yoga'.
"I don't have time for dinner ~ unless it's on the dance floor"
"I've seen a lot of very skinny Indians"
"I'll give yu Puja instead of Shreddies!"
*

They're all right at the time
Surreal Rickshaw Honeymoons to Lonar Meteor Crater Motel.
Accepting the unrestricted, non delusional, full version of me.
"Ex Israeli Prime Minister Gen. Ariel Sharon (Remember him?)
Put in a permanent vegetative state for more than five years!"
"A girl child is someone else's wealth around here."
It's forbidden to have fun; heresy, to be free to be me.
Let's pretend to have Fun, they can't even enjoy that!
It's not these men's fault, only livin' out their DNA!
*

Got to give her Ignition!
Executed on TV for sucking another's cock ~ in the town square!
It's their system, still King's Rule, crushing his subjects' heads with
the Royal Elephant; Fuckin' diabolical! Torture Chambers with new
Stretch machines, your own guillotine dropping on your bent neck!
Hell's scorching flames and hissing geese snapping at your Penis!
Absolutely Unacceptable for slaves & Torture Prisons to still exist!
Against All Our Human Rights; Ultimately we're fighting for these!

"It's Free ~ beautiful visuals Soft Secrets"
3D Psychedelic Porn; Have a look, 'Cats smoking Crack'.
"I want to be Open ~ Fearless, thank you; And Conscious!"
*'They want mastery over third dimensional Time * Space'*
Broadcasting their programs for a Collective Conscious...
We are part of their diabolical manifestation and the rest!
Resonating with ~ tuning to whichever reality frequency.
What is the PERCEPTION of Global existence that you have?
What have you been told to do with your Creative Vibrations?
'Never leave food in plastic, excretes female hormonal estrogen'
*

Beauty's Playa
Never seen so many gorgeous girls on a naturist beach before.
Creating more, seeing you're evolving, evolving; it's just we're not!
Happy Dragons, Kundalini winged serpents, light interfacing ~
between consciousness and matter. Crossing the bridge from
living to dead, removing the veil between inner ~ outer worlds.
Dancing with entheogenic molecules, holding a flower of life.
Dionysus took me by the hand to see my God's eye.
Full of light ~ we are the Universe aware of itself
*

Not Thinking
Opening a new panorama inside connecting to true nature.
"Really now it's Time for me to stop the recreational drugs"
Not wasted, looking after myself ~ to be essentially who I am.
Allow it to happen, without doubting it; Open Reflecting our Space.
Sub Conscious(beliefs) Processing 40 million neural pulses/sec.
Conscious Mind processes only 40 neural impulses per second.
Expect A Golden Age of Aquarius, expect Nirvana ~ bright eyes.
'Are you taking 100% responsibility for what you are experiencing
in your reality'

We're All a Path of Open Space
Apps; Digital Recorder; What Kind of Zen Buddhist am I today?
Doesn't matter where you are, it's acting in your mind ~ lost in Space
Some people need to go to a Holy place
maybe yu get eaten by a crocodile ~
And it doesn't mean anything!
"That's Not True!" Whooshhhhhhh
"Once it's gone it's gone"
'Just Is Grace'

*

Isis' Cupid
Talisman evoking meaning ~ "Wasn't it clear from the start?"
"Allowance, appreciation, it didn't have the edited DNA to break out!
Now the curtains are Open, I can see everything" ~ Divinely.
Very good deeds, considerate to people, smiling, beauty in your face.
Don't follow me and question it all ~ Feel what resonates in Yourself.
An Avatar doing the symbology & Astrology by her Yoni's own light.
A runner meditating, 200 miles in a trance to the next Temple.
"I was the only Tibetan in Manchester that time"
"I paid for a return ticket and where's the bus!?
Lobsang Ray shining at the Potala
"Is it very visual?" ~ "Very Happy!"

*

Holistic Dolmens
Entering into meditation ~ bridging inner * outer worlds.
Directing subtle energies, Universal Yantras of our fractal world.
What happened to the birth right of those Pre Columbians?
Everyone on the Planet ~ beyond duality of name & form.
A higher state of Consciousness, removing all resistance ~
Awakening your Crown chakra, sparkling with a Solar disk.
1000 petalled Lotuses blossoming in the garden of Akasha

In a Ring of 33 Planets
"Everything for the best; All in One ~ with Mama Earth"
Cosmic communication ~ tuning to the Crop Circles.
Seeing the new otherwise we're clinging....
Send me some sexy pictures and Solar flares!
She comes for Sexual Healing basically
Many aspects of that soul mate you find in others.
'A Star is a Star a Planet is a Planet'
'A Planet is born out of a Star'
Gleaming in the Love Crystal.
Transmuting your being*ness
with Love frequency sparkles ~
A trillion diamonds twinkling in you

*

Within Crystal Pressure
"Ketamine is taking over the World!"
"Every soul is a child of the Divine"
'In it to win it' ~ 'It is what it is'.
She's holding the frequency up!
"If you want to be an actress
You have to fulfill your dreams"
Krishna here, Krishna there,
Krishna everywhere ~

*

Biochemical Warfare!
'60% of prisoners in jail in UK. have ADHD!' What's that about?
In the hands of those with no Conscience of empathic Feelings!
White teeth appearing in the dark by the local ATM machine...
They Absolutely shot 20 children in the school playground.
God gave us all the right to eat & drink, reaping what you sow!
Put it away! Blow Back...

The Dalek Lama

"There's a difference in finding yourself on Acid or losing it!"
"That's where the bastards are hanging out all these years!"
'For Your Own Protection Do Not Wear a Crash Helmet
at the CASH Machine' Thank You; Figure that one out!
False friends making you feel important as long as the Coke's
coming in. If you got Coke in your pocket, It's a Gram a fuck!
If you're abusing it ~ side effects > Manic depression!
Keeping Volcanoes in harmony, feeling humble, insignificant.
Matrixians living in the white house! Need an Alien Complex.
'Motivated by unconditional Love * being Free and Fearless'.
"If it makes your heart sing, whatever your conditioning says
Jump through a Portal > "I don't see anything that's Not God"
On the verge of our Collective Consciousness for the next eons
we'll be swimming & bathing in that clear lagoon of ecstatic Bliss.
A Tipping point ~ water from one bowl spilling over into the next.
Quarrel all you like the Love takes over ~ tweaking your wet lips

*

"Go beyond the programs" ~ India Untouched ~ 'Double speaking'

What does the Venus Project say about FREE LOVE ENERGY?
I have met a Yellow Solar Star with a wife, children & mortgage.
Sacred symbols in the language of Light ~ Synchronicity buds.
Red Earth opening up your DNA ~ Being in the Love frequency
Reading 'The Theory and Practice of Oligarchcal Collectivism'
'The Economic Drain Theory' ~ "We Are Dead Mr. Goldstein."
"lots of doctors work in Babylon ~ they don't all live in Babylon"
Only way to Rule is to Divide ~ Internet is bringing us together.
Building our Temples there ~ in our thoughts ~ how it all moves
from the opening in your heart ~ to a holographic Cosmic Ray.
'Going up as high as possible by helping the lower ones get up.'
Pandora flew out of her box forever
Pinnacles of creative essence ~

More Years of Italian Lead!
Fed. forced Banks to be Predatory lenders! Their Solution to life?
Consequences of International Settlements Bank, Basel, Switzerland!
A Holocaust of Credit Default Swaps; Another Final Solution!
Sensing Opportunities ~ "Control them or they'll Control you!"
Wants Risk, excitement, freedom, yet don't have any discipline,
Concentration. Who wants that Responsibility & Commitment?
Addicted to the High, Lows, her characteristics, the Sensations!
Enjoying the buzz, the Attention, habit, feeding its own lifestyle.
Don't wanna change it! You're Intelligent, experienced, aware.
Let it go ~ to be freer
*

Keeping the Truth
Teenage nymphs censored for fear of seeing their own breasts.
Innocence ~ No Logic of ~ get in the ecstasy mood.
'Can't compare one shit with another shit, they're both shit'
And throw the Pain out ~ we are all Loved not made in FEAR.
Up for all the good energy ~ hoping it might rub off...
White Crystals at Sunrise ~ "Vipers don't come in Yellow"
*

Nuts in a Hood!
Thrown into the well of Zamzam, chanting Dark side of a Moon.
Mouth kissing an extraterrestrial rock star, Invading Crusaders.
Sound is a Vibration ~ bit of black concrete or a rosy lingham?
A drug store on every corner ~ Dysfunctional, greedy Capitalism.
Who are the Predators, Creditors that own all this debt, how come
Goldman Sachs' Bank's getting away with this & whose bank is it?
Ask Standard Charter, HSBC about Money Laundering for Mafias.
Barclay's illegally fixing interest rates, GlaxoSmithKline for selling
drugs to children knowing they're useless; Profit promoting suicide.
Justice gives them a fine, for rich Corporate gangsters no jail time!

Searching Light

Wanting to convey Extreme feelings in her works of ART.
Which Programs do you want to unleash inside your Mind?
Do you understand the basic meaning of human Truth friend?
Or do you want to be an Ostrich with his head buried in the sand?
Reconnecting with reality, stars glistening in the desert night sky.
Mind body Spirit ~ using colours to paint expressions of Philosophy.
Using the right hemisphere of your brain to open the gates of Love.
It's Creative Art not Politics, Economics, Psychology or Sociology!
Is your stream of consciousness flowing in the Ocean of humanity?
Have the freedom, the courage to enter into this deep ecstatic state.
Have the faith to stand up to the demons, in fields of radiant energy.
Where do you want to go in this crystalline Caravanserai of Life?
Surrendering ~ recovering, total Immersion in your heart.
"Shake it loose and let it fall"

*

More Shanti than Gandhi

"Just loved it on MDMA; You do don't you!?" ~ More Feelings.
"I'm always happy when I see a Cosmic postcard on a tree"
Insight all up or down ~ We're just meditating on the eternal.
In between the words is Space where magic is invisibly flowing.
You're the enlightened one because you recognize the truth!
You are the miracle ~ I have seen so much magic in my life,
means 'get out of the way!' Don't believe in Identification again.
Relax so the other can Relax ~ just getting in the love frequency.
Putting your energy into it, free of it ~ It's all Magic, I'm innocent,
I wanna believe in miracles too; Implosion ~ 'Intent becomes reality'
We're just consciousness, hairy & spiritual, experience in human form.
*Here to Learn, we're all Spiritual fractals * energy gathering clusters.*
There's the Givers and there's the Takers ~
And there's all those in ~ between Spaces

<u>You Are what's lookin' at it!</u>
Seeing I'm Not the Bottle, I'm here witnessing it!
If you can see it ~ realize You Are Not It.
You're the consciousness ~ allowing the thing to happen.
My God I am that Space ~ transcended the Identity
telling me I am in Pain or I am in Pleasure.
Now it's all sensation in the Universe
Not calling Pain by any name, by any illusion.
'Mine' separates you from the whole thing ~
My baby, my body, my life, myself, my active Mind.
It's Not like that ~ Objects with all the attachments!
Getting all the Illusions from those thought concepts.
Burning up the Mind burns the Identity, the Ego, the Id.
It doesn't matter, there's no matter of the matter you see.
The Unmanifest is always permanent the Manifest temporary.
Mirroring a brain, neurons infinitely smaller than a grain of sand.

*

<u>Moksha Motel</u>
It is You ~ Life Itself ~ ONE IS FORMLESS.
Symbols, Soap Operas, Backup App. Baba.
Colour Blast "They haven't got the right God!"
Representation ~ Life is all in the creativity.
God is Life Eternal not talking Disney characters.
Not the Mickey Mouse myth, don't get more confused!
They get lost in the finger pointing ~ it's not in the representation of it,
believing your finger is the Moon ~ only Your self can go to the Moon.
A dog looking at the Master when he's already thrown the stick!
Absence of the Sun light ~ we've turned away from it!
Manic Massage, 'Church' ~ 'The blind leading the blind'
"I'd have Venus ~ evoking her from a fountain of bliss"
In the dark you need a light to see

Golden Frequency

Golden light, Golden Lingham, Golden Yoni.
Go out of your normal way and let it go ~
"I didn't know Space because of the Control"
Everyone has their Unique crystal ~ let it shine
In the Experience with the light of Creation ~
Transmuting, transmitting the Crystal ~ tuning it in.
You're in Space when you are free ~
We're all fuckin' Slaves, we enslave ourselves
by listening to the Ego programming Conditioning us.
In that Freedom of Love ~ All Is Feeling.
We're living in the frequency anyhow ~ we make the blockages!
"Everything Is Fine as Long as Everything Is"

*

Get on with what you got for the Best

How do you switch off ~ my mind; Not thinking, more Clear Mind.
Being more the Space, Accepting, detached, Silent In Meditation ~
Instead of defining all these moments of existence see what happens
To touch, see, believe the light; Keeping on the path separates you!
Staying on the path, step off the path ~ into the whole Spaciness
Infinite permutations going on ~ we accept it as that...
Not the Karma drama ~ that Universal resonance too!
"I Love this Idea of multi * dimensional Cosmic energy"
Stars beyond stars beyond stars beyond stars * So now
"I Keep being attached to reality by my ankhlet!"

*

Mind * Form

Really Just a Car but you Identify it as Your/My CAR; Attachment!
More Aware becoming Balanced ~ Life Conscious emptiness' Form.
Resonating, noting stillness, Silence ~ Keep focusing, infinite Space
around everything ~ Connecting with Love feeling in a state of Grace

Just this^Hook!

That's what they're doing to us, keeping us believing in Thinking ~
The Mind Identity ~ Your Ego taking over the essential realization of
Space is Consciousness ~ in tnere is the true sense of who we are.
Keeping us rattling around in cur Minds, heeding their Propaganda,
which is a means to Control our*selves and the other 7 billion of us!
What do they train us to think of ~ that theirs is the reasoning to be.
Formulating structure of who we are ~ who we are supposed to be.
Ask the Vatican or Queen, the Ordained Authorities for an Identity!
And we follow all their directives, the Dictator sucking up the Power!
Without this 'Id' you're left witn only the Space that you want to be!
"flowing in the I don't know"

*

Mental * Space

'Mirage on the horizon of Brahma'
"We are nothing ~ I am nothing * it's all an Illusion > Nothing there"
Because it's all put together Inside the Brain ~ Our Visual field.
Deluded to think that we are separate to the Living Soil matrix.
Dispossessing our cousins the Orangutan's living there!
Thanks a lot for this Hallucinatory landscape!
'It's All coming from Heaven' Oh Yeah!
"I need a woman who understands ~
the deepness and the freeness"
Resonation ~ "The Meteor is coming on Friday"
"Nothing to eat but my clothes and Tarot cards!"
"I Don't Do Yoga"

*

OMNI * ENERGY*NEERS
"STOP * INTERRUPTING ~ THE TRANCE!"
'The Lightest Footprint on the Planet'
The Best Way of Looking at Life ~
"Trees are very cool"

Dolphin * Endorphin

As if the natural richness of Thailand is not enough they have ~
to throw their youngest daughters into this Faustian sex bargaining.
In a land of Golden Palaces; where is their Aspire*rational Mind Sire?
Rising above the Ignorance and greedy ego, debauchery, apathy,
atrophy, agony, melancholy, slavery ~ to Living in loving harmony?
In Solitary Confinement ~ She cut his tongue with a sharp bamboo!

*

Sinister Wallpaper

Let's try Happy a dimension within chaotic dualities; Not Gruesome.
Who's threatening You? Keeping Troops Happy on Fuhrer Strasse!
Official Approval, dictating who goes up and who goes into the pit!
Play the Romantic Symphony mate! Let's escape to fantasy don't
need any more immeasurable destruction from your Black Holes!
Art therapy for a traumatized Nation; You allowed this to happen,
No one's going to let you Forget ~ what no one wants to remember!
Need an army of Bricklayers to build that Berlin WALL of Separation
Physical manifestation ~ who disfigured her face with a Blow Torch?
'What's the nature of Art coming out of the ruins of a World War?'
It is the worst Crime Against Humanity and how do we react to it?
Began the systematic surveillance of the Planet, made up Paranoia!
No Place to Hide ~Taking No Prisoners, Puts them all to the Sword!
"This Must Not Happen Again ~ Another Heritage of Terror"
!!!!!!!!!!!!Emitting Radioactivity!!!!!!!!!!!!!!!

*

L'ADORED

"I should do that more often put my wings out"
We should All be wearing a Crown!
So Enchanted by her beauty ~
"Is the Passion still Alive in You?"
Putting it into Practice Baby

The Hidden Symbolism
"I love taking drugs at Alton Towers!"
That's what they call Ket ~ 'Hippy Crack'
Some people never look up at sky high
Consumed inside the Matrixcal allegory!
"Are they taking the piss on the News or what,
7.7 It was the secret Government that did it!"
How do these people Rule the World today?
She's at the Top, they have their own Agenda!
As long as you don't believe them, that's their end game!
If you believe in the Truth they'll extraordinarily render you too!
Not realizing anything, keeps you asleep, tuning masses into X Factor
The News, Coronation Street, Cum dancing, It's all there for a reason!

*

"Wake Up!"
"He's on his 3rd renunciation of a renunciation, then renunciates again-
of everything! What's it all about? Rule #1~ BE HAPPY ~ Space bliss
Religion needs to be dropped, by default accept another Religion!
"The Pope made a good move ~ Now fuck off before we lock you up!"
Admit it and redistribute all the wealth they've ripped off ever since!
"Nothing benefits the World as much as a man
who is beyond making a Profit" ~ Maharaj...
No more pretending about anything, got the Proof!
Feeling the sea spray ~ sounds of the wild geese.
Takes you on the trip ~Try the 'do nothing'
just be it; feel the Space ~ He's probably right.
Need enough of Potential to avoid suffering ~
A solar roof, vortex turbine, spring well water.
At the beginning of the Flowers of Life ~
Lining up all the right crystals.
You are ~ we are, Perfect

*Kandinsky's * Blue Riders*
Plasma Baba ~ Like it hot & Sticky but not too sticky!
Let Universal Space work for you ~ Energy Company.
*Don't 'Do' meditation ~ You realize that You Are*It.*
'Fussy 'bout my Honey'
*

*Open * Heart*
Keeping the Love forever ~
Hard to reconcile Torture ~ away from all this Brainwashing.....
Borderline personality disorders, Defence Mechanism technique,
'Maharaja Mirage' Role behaviour ~ "We have to shoot someone!"
The Authority, Power, those on Top of everyone else.
They definitely don't want to lose it ~ so we can all get a fair share!
Everyone had a hard time, over feeling suffering ~ thru to the Bliss.
It depends ultimately on You
*

Breathalyser before Peptides
"You seem in a very good mood!" ~ "Blow into this!"
"I've only had a couple of beers but don't feel very well officer"
My baby screamed off at the last Island on the left in a red Cadillac
The Riot van pulled up!
*

Cosmic Dust
"You come from another Star"
And now you've come to Earth ~
Expressionism of a Celestial seed…
Free Mind to be Open ~ a sacred happening
And I'm longing for that ~ "to be in it or Not to be in it" ~ Being.
Cocoon of light ~ fuelled with Love energy from the Crystal grid.
Over the Sun's explosions we get more and more light!

'It's a Mind Field'
Being Open ~ All going on Inside there.
Listening to the silence ~ Inner stillness.
"Thinking makes me stay in the duality"
In the Mind; Switch ~ off mental distraction
It's so simple, that the brain couldn't get it ~
can't perceive the silence through the white noise!
Illusion, what seems Real, Isn't! Simply be stillness.
Getting out the Mental is Eternal

*

Mind Fucked
Being Mental ~ Looking for Ourselves is making the Duality.
When there's nothing more there ~ You're Self Aware.
Seeking for the Spirit ~ when You Are The Spirit!!!!
While you're feeling your body you're Not Thinking.
Just the PURE FEELING in all of Life ~
Misidentifying with Life ~ is the evil Ego
need for conflict, friction ~ You simply see It!
"Awareness becomes AWARE of Itself ~
when No*thing else Is there to distract it!"

*

It's The Love Miracle
I Notice the Living reality ~ Operating in every Cell.
Pure Intelligence of Not Knowing but Feeling It.
The Mystery and depth of Life; Don't Name It.
We'll put it into an Illusion ~ then materialize it.
"I Am Not That Object ~ I Am Primordial Grace.
We are not what happens ~ You're just IN/SPACE
for what's happening ~ from where it all comes from.
'Nothing to get ~ It's All this FEELING here & now'
"Infinity Is a Singularity not a Duality"

Placebo of a Vow
The Power of the Mind <> Zero Space frequency of Love.
Nothing is intrinsically Black or white ~ infinite reflections.
It could have been anything, who knows what it is?
"They didn't want to come and play your game!"
"She's a carpenter on fire ~ nice but not deep"
'Forget Madness come on a Cruise'
Going for Inspirational FUN ~
You've gotta have the dream!
"I really wanted to be a hippy!"
forever in forever's ~ stream

*

Happiness * Nirvana
"I've had enough Suffering ~
Framing of Space * it's not the Colonnades, the Obelisks, the Temples
Subject's deluded by the material Objects not the essential Space ~
In this Space is the Pure * Consciousness ~ energy that never dies!
"You're not praying for one or the other, you're looking for the door"
"Maybe they Hallucinated it ~ they see what they want to see"
A lot believe the voices in their head is God talking to them ~
It's their Own Mind talking ~ "None of it is Real"
You're seeing the 7 dimensional thing in your brain
You haven't gone anywhere ~ It's in your own cells,
deep Purple energetic fields, Yellow auras of the Sun.
What Spirits are you talkin' bout, it's in your own head.
The blue white translucent Angel or goblin from Hell?
They're sacrificing humans ~ what you tryin' to say!
Do you really wanna be a Mayan sacrificial, High Priestess?
Psychopathic drugs, cutting beating hearts out of people!
You're a Flip Out!

Jupiter's Sun flares
Turning Duality's Power Switch, ON, Off ~
"You can only eat so many chocolates"
Intuitive touch, Extra Alluring Tendency ~
Resonating with a sensitive kitty from Arcturiano,
It's a Love Star, it's quite bright, she's dynamite!
Getting hotter, seeing shadows more and more ~
Alchemy standing in the fire ~ Burn it, Transmute it!
More Venus ~ transmuting emotions over the Heart
to the Higher Chakra They have lived on the root.
Harmony is all round you ~ In the Sunlight.
By acknowledging nature Spirit You Love It
*

Crystal Salad
Shiva Cocktail ~ Integrating numbers
You can use the Mind, there for that.
Controlling ourselves ~ over time.
When you think of the future it has hooked you!
Concept of linear time ~ only BE the Present.
"You don't know what's around the corner!"
I like leaving the future Open ~ that's New!
I wanna give her the juiciest juice for free.
*Singing Archangel arias*buzzing of a Bee*
*

Star People
"There's a Sun in the Earth!"
Tibetan Portals, Jerusalem's Gates, shut.
Yellow aura frequencies ~ filtering it out,
left with different signals, light energies.
Old rainbow brother traveling in Space.
If you feel Love ~ that's all you want

23

'This Is The Lie'
First lie is the 'Separation' then Lie after lie after lie ~
Over everything ~ Around us is Love filled up & Life.
The flow of Love ~ frequency being of the in-between Space.
Choosing which frequency ~ we want without the projections,
reflections of the Mind stuff by Allowance of how it Is.
Making a definition IS Separating ourselves from the Love ~
Get the whole stream when you are connected to the One in all ~
Unconditional Love ~ not 'See Something Say Something' Big Bro'
Can't support a lie because connected to the Wholeness ~
We all have to fall through the gateway of Grace & Mercy

*

Blue White Light
For ourselves, we have to forgive Ourselves (not others) as we
have to forgive Ourselves for what we did during the Separation!
"I go now to the Angel Centre" ~ Keeping it Real.....
"Took everything, left the SIM cards lined up on the steps!"
Looking ~ listening to the inner silence ~ stillness

*

The people waking up
It's through Us Not the State! 'VIVE LES PETITS LAPINS ~
"We've reached a point where we get our POWER BACK!"
"The small puzzle is coming together as a picture"
They put you in this BOX with the Intent to Control You ~ Your Life!
"Jesus is a Terrorist" to many so is the Dalai Lama; I AM Psychedelic.
What cookie have you got in your brain, which microchip in your arm?
Motive, one Wo/Man's Terrorist Is another Wo/Man's Freedom Fighter.
All small steps, today stopped Cosmetic Tests on Rabbits in Europe.
*** See Yourself as a Multi ~ Dimensional Being ***
Taking their POWER and Not telling them what to do!
"I'm in the Mind like you"

Sacred Geometry

"They're so tuned into this Caste System ~
they'd fight you and kill you to maintain it!"
Spirit Imprint ~ Blueprint of the Gods.
'We are the Sparks' ~ It's burning!
Taking on our part in a Magical way

*

Heart Identity

That common Link, No tags, Labels.
Seeing IT AS IT IS ~ Light of Space,
too incredible to put a name to it!
It's like Tripping. putting a name to it,
don't need that! Inspiration of creation
Love is everywhere ~ it's all around
Without naming it.......Very True....
It's like it is because we call it so ....
It's Love because we call it Love ~
That which I see with my eyes is LOVE

*

Spiritual Nature

Our Programming of Massive Conditioning.
How aware are YOU of the LIVING ~ SACRED
thing such as Geese flying South ~ Senses of the Forest?
Seeing it ONLY for what they can get out of it, Exploitation!
What's the cost, what's the profit, what's their bottom line?
Chopping all the trees ~ reducing our experience of LIFE!
They don't care, are Unaware, Ignorance is their Mind set.
Forgive them if you can because they have no feeling for you.
"To be Conscious of Life or not to be Conscious of Life?"
They've reduced it to an 'Object' ~ no empathy for its being

Pharaoh Sun Zen

Siemens, the Big Corporations, Our Holy Cows and they're Enslaving Us!
'Spirituality and artistic creation is the same energy used in a different way
Yoni ~ that's a sacred part! "I once poured milk over a Lingham!"
Bursting time ~ lines, 'It's not in the doing ~ it's Being in being'
Like when you try to wake up a Zombie, can't do any better
than to chop its head off, leave it in its Peace, Peace.
Don't let it break your Faith... All in the holding it up ~
if you think in the right direction everything will happen.
Now Mother Earth is deciding, she has already gone through
the Cosmic Centre ~ 26* Sagittarius

*

Agent's Laws

We don't want and shall not have any Velvet Revolutions here! Da!
She had it All under control, it was bliss, bliss, bliss, bliss, bliss, bliss.
Everyone got the Love energy * chakra, Open ~ heart.
'You're on it or you're Not on it' ~ Don't have to THINK about it too much.
It's All In The Mind ~ it's Not an Illusion, it's a Real Point to realise.
Not in the driver's seat ~ sitting in the passenger back seat,
looking at it and Enjoying it as a Movie passing by.
If you have to give it up ~ be Inactive!
'Unconditional Love ~ Is All Over'

*

FEAR ~ 'False Evidence Appearing Real'

We're everywhere ~ every moment * Now You Are Here.
She's actually on Venus transmitting quantum energy through her.
Mind Controlling Programming. The Hulk, Sexy Vampires, Horrors!
If monkeys come on your roof, get a Stick or throw some mangoes ~
This Terror happens every day need the Shock, catalyst of awareness!
It's another Demon, sucking emotions out of the people, feeding on us.
They live on our emotions, just gobbling it all up ~
Pope in the Vatican owns 26% of Global Wealth!
'The more enlightened ~ the dark has to go'

'Let sleeping dogs lie'
Creating a safe place inside ~
Making a dream for the traumatized, abused.
It's all about the Mind ~ feeling the Absolute.
"Your Mind gives it to us if you want"
Fear makes the World very small ~
Free choice ~ choose the all enriching.
Exploring the goodness ~ Perceptions of goals.
Can't have enough well being ~ balanced in nature.
Self experience of what is there....

*

Can be too much
Being in an extreme situation ~
"You Love someone else!"
"If you don't Love Yourself ~
HOW CAN YOU Love someone else?"
She's deep in the fearful & Insecurity,
clinging to something for her reality ~
"It's about Negative Stress Regulation"
"They used a hot poker and melted his testicles!"
How much Torture can you stand?

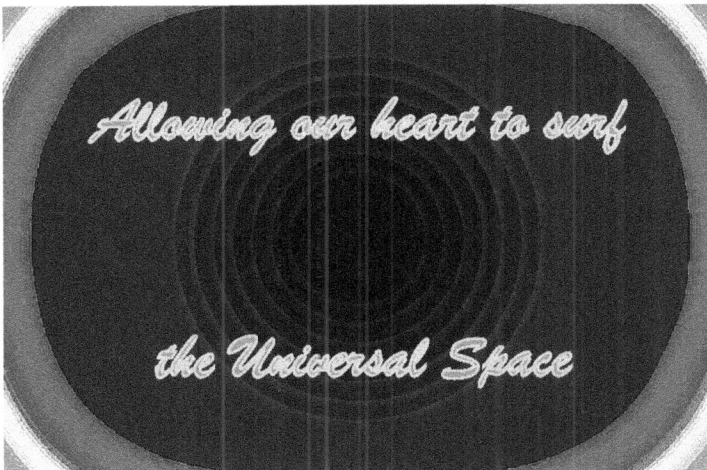

Allowing our heart to surf

the Universal Space

'Goa Planning Dept'

"Life is so grim without a chillum"
"That's a good job being someone's fan!"
Vishnu ~ Is No Poison.. but purest Nectar!
Lakshmi's Blessings ~ you have to Please her.
Not only CASH can bring you happiness ~
Magical numbers on paper ~ suddenly aware nothing is yours!
Even the body will dissolve into the elements ~ then you realize
sitting in a crematorium on the burning Ghats and it's very Shanti,
You are a soul not a body ~ you have to leave the body one day
Free Spirit through the Purity

*

Pasha Flash & 21 Green Taras

"Wherever he walked Lotus flowers grew"
The last resort ~ praying to the Blue Buddha.
"It's not every time you take Acid you're gonna see Shiva!"
"OM MANI PADMA HUM" ~ "OM MANI PADMA HUM"

*

Flower Shower

Sit in the Limousine and enjoy the ride from now on!
It will all fall into place ~ You are the Observer.
Otherwise you'd never see it unfolding ~
The one where we all come from ~ so we can Trust.
It becomes more beautiful when you taste the Cream

*

Chillum Castle

Kali's daughters ~ I guess they get burnt a lot.
Lemon Soda even Magician's drink it in India ~ Tantric rituals.
"If you see a lemon in the middle of the road don't touch it ~
hang it on the door with chilies against the evil eye."
"They have to change with the times ~
otherwise you'll be a museum piece"

All the Time Uploading
'The 13th Amendment to Abolish Slavery' "Fuck Off!"
"When they Stop the drugs they Stop the music"
"As I started to move out ~ he started to flip out!"
Kali's Power ~ "In the end I dance on Shiva"
"I can look in everybody's eyes and see ~ Love"
Exploring their Psyches ~ "It's hot, the Flame!"

*

Ultra Surreal Ganesh
His mind began to wander as if he were about to lose his senses.
Giving themselves up in complete ~ unashamed nakedness. OK.
Krishna, Parvati and Hanuman stars in India's new Easy Rider!
Head to toe, proper skin, hemp trunk on purple Acid.
So bad it brings up your compassion of acceptance ~
Indian Futuristic Mythology of hallucinatory fascination.
It's Hampi Dude, Bangalore Dude, Allahabad Dude.
"It'll give her something to do in the wet season"
"I can't get it Baba ~ then it came"

*

Giraffe Trousers
"I didn't know you could do that"
"I'm very good at selling people Shit."
'Braveheart was hard enough ~ Hung, drawn and quartered!'
Here comes the blonde with the Hula hoop and pink hotpants.
Frontline ~ "We're fighting the Chemical War!"

*

Youtopia ~ The Berlin Touch
"I knew him when I was Brenda"
"It doesn't make sense ~ The Drug Is You!"
Rainbows coming through the window pane.
The Heart Opening ~ Psychetropic not misanthropic...
Looking in the fire concentrated on the shadow of the Sun.
Transmutation of the elements

Water Snakes
Seeing yourself in all the reflections ~ in new now, cut-off.
No one knows ~ just accept all of it, in the things as we are.
Not in the Judgment ~ No Divisions; the Discernment, Gnosis.
'The Knowledge, the receiving of the knowledge ~ the Knower'
Freedom in the discerning ~ you don't have to choose this or that.
All choices are made with the Illusion of having a choice ~
"If you do not have a choice how can you choose?"
"If you don't look right or left ~ you get run over by a cow!"
Who's accepting everyone as Perfekt ~ in whatever you do?
Exchanging a high dimensional Eco level ~ frequency.
Making any judgment freely ~ "Isn't that a demand?"
"No a wish for yourself ~ take it or leave it, it's up to you
And Love Yourself!"
*

The Russian Connection
Being in contact ~ "the bhajis are good in Chapora"
Chocolate Peyote tasting strong at the Kumbh Mela!
She is so explicit, defensive, demands this Attention,
In doubt, feeling accused, asked her a simple question.
"Need one ant to tell the other ants ~ there's the honey"
"Big vacuum cleaners on Andromeda sucking up Chem. trails ~
then they throw 'em in Black Holes ~ Really funky stuff, out of it."
It's comin' out now ~ Power Mad Lizzies!
*

Red Velvet Flares Being in Paradise
Owning it ~ having Awareness, knowing, the Senses ~ chewing it!
"Sat with a massive San Pedro in San Francisco ~ is it worth it?"
Respect for Cabenzas, "We're all loving it in harmony ~ You know"
No need of a Visa for an eccentric artist of Bohemia, so he thought!
"Lots of people took LSD especially your 60's hippy generation"
High in the sky ~ Public Address; "Don't Touch the Opaque Acid!"

Touchdown

"Go crazy but respect other people's space." Oh! Mum & dad;
"He's fuckin another woman in front of me on our Honeymoon"
"He's your husband get on with it girl!" Indebted servitude dowry!
"These Indian guys don't understand the concept of 'NO!'"
"Fuck off and don't swear at me." Changing female's inferiority!
Drunken uncle parties and confused hen nights at Shiva Valley!
She's off our hands! "Accidentally I slapped your arse, Sorry"
"OK that's where you draw the line!"
"It comes to an end at some time...
I've got my brothers in Bihar!"
Gotta catch them early ~

*

Silicon Tipped Valleys

"When you give slaves freedom ~
they don't know what to do with it!"
"Here's your Palace back & the cake!"
Bringing back Madame Guillotine, svp!
Came in the house and they washed his feet ~
had a Persian carpet on the floor and servants.
I read 'The Prophet' ~ 3 days at the beach on Acid.
Tears came to my eyes.

*

Ego & Conditioning

'Beauty is in the eye of the beholder' & all else.
Birth and death ~ two sides to the same coin.
Strange how one is revered and one feared!
Wouldn't this be a perfect moment to die?
You don't want Mossad after you ~ Landing
a deadly droning assassin over your head!
Burning witches at the steak, slowly BBQing.
Don't need to take us to the Torture Chamber ~
Sending invisible beams into your bed ~ DEAD!

<u>Learning from our Discernment to it.</u>
"When did you realize that you fell out of loving me?"
"Why do we have such a bad impression of Duality?"
Now we're out of that Power Game, fed with 'blah, blah, ba, ba, ba'
Who is still manipulated by their negative frequencies? Say cheese!
Filling Your head with Non Stop, illusions of THINKING for this/that.
Which is fine up to a point ~ always remember the energetic spaces.
Trapped like a Rat on a Matrix WHEEL of THOUGHT but it's all only
spiraling chiaroscuro energies ~ you are its dissociated Realisation.
'Sat Chit Anand' ~ other nice words to contemplate on; Try 'Unity'
Made the wings out of wax but they melted in the Sunshine.
"Year of the Tiger and I'm only a horse in a Vortex!"
*

<u>"What Shall I Say to a Mirage?"</u>
She did Tai Chi ~ flowing all night
Follow your feeling ~ be ultimately.
Accept other perceptions of reality.
Not thinking, rationalizing any judging ~
the busy, competitive, materialist World.
Not this Religious, superstition Kingdom.
Not just Imagination ~ but the realization;
senses being in momentary awareness.
Your Zero Spatial Consciousness Is Alive
*

<u>Like a Black Magic Place</u>
Uber Massive Psychological Warfare On Us!
Playing into somebody's Sociopathic hands.
At least, simply have to witness it. ~ At Best!
I suspect many things ~ We're trying to work
out the Truth to those Diametrically Opposed.
Who's lying to us and who's not lying to us?
Confused people because ~ Made to THINK!

Tibetan Silver Birds
You would be charged with GBH in GB!
Hugging a Police wo/man, that's a good one.
Your biggest weapon is True Forgiving ~
You have to be better than them ~ A Cosmic Architect.
Making the most of the misery ~ Kissing your Torturer!
Do it in your 'No Mind' Awareness energy spinning around you.
Allowance is the Key, you are just the Projection of his anger!
Giving yourself another World for you to have an example of
a picture of what you don't want to learn! Nothing gets lost ~
Just Surrender to it, enjoying Life ~ Unconditional Love Space
*

Universal Radio
Solar Consciousness ~ Exotic flowers & Flares!
New Intelligence jumping to the lovely channels.
We can go where we want to ~ projecting in Space.
Tuning into Awareness ~ It's already happening.
If you don't eat it you don't know how it tastes.
*Falling in the Cosmic pudding * where you Kill Reality!*
You have your sacred geometric Triangle then you let it go.
Aligning the 1,2,3 lower chakras ~ igniting the Love fuel.
Allowing the Space to occur for a White cloud of Spirit.
Bringing them up into the three higher chakras.
5th dimensional Space ~ All is in the FEELING
*

*Mantra * Tantra * Yantra*
Shakti's the dream of Brahma ~ being All in Oneness.....
"Solar photon light hits our DNA and makes y/our Hologram"
How do I begin to see it all as an Illusion of duality ~ reality!
Gymnast's luminous Death Mask at a Chinese Chaos Circus.
Beautiful moving in the Sublime ~ Grace.
Beyond the horizontal of All concepts.

"It's Not My Debt!"

Dream streaming, coming from a deep well ~
Shade for the Baba ~ No shadow at night.
What is Illusion, in his heart ~ with the music.
Things are up and things are down ~
the Sunshine beaming through you.
"I saw the lies constantly ~ Aware!"

*

E's * Pills

Local Football derby, "I Love you brother ~
Won't Stanley blade you anymore!"
Changed a generation ~ Revolution.
'All Twinkled Up'

*

Four Tour Corporate Mercenary!

"We are there to WAGE War Not WIN War!"
"When I killed my first person.. saw his eyes"
More dying in non combat than active combat.
Suicides of non Veterans overtaken the Veterans!
PTS. ~ profundity like being on an acid trip man!
They ruined, destroyed so many people.
'Young, dumb and full of cum'

*

Source to Source

Crashing waves ~ starting a new feeling ~ soft landing.
'Having the Opportunity of the Freedom ~ of/from the money'
"You will break my heart" ~ was that her first guilt trip, in disguise?
I'd never want to do that! "Give me an Independent woman any time"
They wanna have FUN ~ yet you've made yourself Unattainable!
It's All two carat gold plated down at the Central Vault!
And always having a little Hitler above you!
She's being with you for the right reasons ~

TANTRIC TEMPLAR

The King's making all the nicest young women pregnant!
They come out in the Spring for better survival. 'Let's go Surfin ~
Her body's a dream ~ You know it's not you, it's coming through you!
Breathtaking experiment ~ Celebrating the intimate & sensual.
'The emotional power when she met one of her former Slaves'
"What You do for You becomes You" ~ Vessel of Consciousness.
Transmitting so much Selflessness ~ Giving the Blessing

*

She's a Metaphor for an Erotic Meteorite!

No Apsaras here ~ Not being driven to distraction!
"Space is Full ~ Starsrips are waiting to come down!"
Concentrate on your own level ~ just getting higher frequency.
Taking on the Karma of the woman you're having multi-orgasms with!
Just on the outside, you only lose ~ she won't let you close to her.
"I don't have the feeling for it ~"

*

Sperm Whale Sandwich or Ganesh Rice Pudding

"Ravenna, Ego; Rama, Pure Consciousness; Sita, devotion to this
Consciousness; Hanuman represents all the animals being God"
The Mind likes that, when it's Self-Righteous ~ just a Mind trip!
Ego kidnaps this Love and devotion ~ then Ego is Conquered!
Don't take the Myths too literally * picnic in the forest at Khirganga.

*

In The Emperor's Dragon Boat

"They've got endless time to listen to your bullshit in India"
That's what they do! Didn't need a cup of Amphetamine coffee
"I'm in the perfect place!" ~ astride a Siberian, Minky with blue eyes.
"I'm always lookin' in my mirrors; No rules, totally different Mind*set!"
Let's have some Science fiction porn, triangulated, back on the grid!
There's got to be Debbie from Dallas! "Even the negatives were cut!"
"It's all around"

Immaculate Deflowering

"I Fear God, I Don't Love God!" A rusty razor blade on her clit!
"Put her in the Fire ~ sent her to the Jungle for twelve years to
prove to us her natural Goddess purity ~ Tried drowning her?"
"We're living in a Laboratory on Mother Earth... Hari Ram"
Shakti unfolding ~ for the witnessing of this manifestation.
To know you're just the Observer of her divine FORM.
Brahma in perfect balance ~ Is It All

*

'The Lustful Tour' ~ In Sticky Air

"No one can be offended by the absolute Truth of Acid"
He encountered the Divine revelation on DMT.
"We're All Part of Nature" ~ "We Are Nature!"
"We're all made from Sunlight in a Cosmic Ocean"
"Searching for the light ~ when We Are the Light!"

*

Somebody had a Good Time!

They knew how to really Torture people; No messing!
"Let's look for the Devil in her burning pubic hair"
'The Church is separating you - from the Divine'
A Con...... in solitary isolation
Divided & Conquered ~
burnt her Magic wand!

*

Cruising in Life ~

"Giving them a Fridge!"
That'll cure them awhile!

*

Totalitarianism Promotion!

When they made MDMA illegal
that was STOPPING HAPPINESS.
Putting them in Prison ~ the end of the line!
"Blow up all dams, Seriously!"

36

'Chai Chillum Chapati ~ Chelo Parvati'
'It's one thing being alive another knowing You Are ALIVE SPACE!'
"No action without consequence' ~ that's a strange coincidence!
'Bombing For Peace' ~ 'Where's all your Gold Idols?"
Blame it on Al Qaeda! Selfish, Corruption and Greed.
27 Congressmen now being prosecuted for rape!
How can you believe in a System like this?
Time for your bamboo massage Mr. Minister!
*

Hot Blessings on Rue Paradise
"You go India, everywhere people dying, lying next to the road!"
In the net surrounded by Tarantulas, getting rid of extra Toxins.
I don't know what that was ~ Psychic*Trance is my language.
Chillin' with an amazing Angel crowd you wouldn't believe!
In the Tantric Temple ~ equality happening of its own accord.
'Women Are Love' ~ for Men to admire & to reflect!
If we see the Love in them we give it back to them;
All Lovers unfolding Communication: It feels great, it is great!
Structure & destruction ~ Shiva * Shakti Is our unique tuning.
We let that make an impression on us ~ live it out of Creation
by itself ~ throwing the pictures from your blissful soul.
Living Freedom, 100,000 petalled Lotuses ~ in bloom
*

All for the Best
Hanging out on Planet MDMA.
Opening up your stars & hearts ~
but if your heart is Open anyway!
Receiving, tuning, connecting, contacting delightful being..
Alignment in yourself with your glowing Crystallised body.
Enthralling and very thrilling sucking juicy petite mangoes.
We need Affirmation ~ sexually stimulating Love food.
My torrid Phallic light ~ bathing in her plane of Uranus' forces.
'Passion with consciousness becoming Unconditional Love'

SUPREMELY SENSUAL

*Positive Reply: You've got the potential and you know how to operate in the best positions ~ synergetic magic * angelic sexual lusciousness gyrating on my delirious, pounding cock. Your tender love is fuelling the passion rocket. You are the full temptation, Venus pleasure girl, driving desire out of its mind. Only true Love is good enough for one such as You * a nymph of bliss dedicating herself to bathing in the Ocean of sincerity, where poets come to lick chocolate cream from your gorgeous, fully equipped body that knows how to enjoy its gifts of pleasure laid before you by Hieros Gamos' of the delight. You are Ishtar's devotee performing subtle arts of consciousness, honouring her own Goddess, my hard phallus dancing inside Dawn's ecstasy.*

*I would like a private viewing of your heart, to feel its beating spirit chanting a mantra to Eros' kiss. You've earned another delicious Sicilian lemon cheesecake ~ for your work is superb, transcribing the hieroglyphics of a clear blue sky. Your offering of the most sublime treasures conjurering hot lascivious anticipations! Happiness is growing with you in supra*sensitivity, making angels wonder at inspirational Love beams bursting deep in Love's petals. Your gentle seductiveness brought us delirious divine succulence. Beyond excess ~ your being is illuminated like a shooting Star as you gaze down into my eyes; I taste your Cosmic juicy fragrances. I smell romance in you like summer's wet dreams ~ licking sweat, honey dripping down your smooth skin. We'll enjoy magical trips together hand in hand. High as butterflies swooning in your sweet irresistible Heaven. Together on another trip, Love that's what it is. Burning life's sacred fire within * makes me hot, makes you moist! Smoking hips ~ Your puffy nipples, hard, erect, throbbing, tingling! Cumming inside her glistening milky way exploding as super Comets! Beautiful people expressing their energetic consciousness & desires. See you in Paradise * blissful moments ~ feeling it happening as It Is.*

Laundering ~ Leverage # Plunder

The Quasi Religious Ruling Oligarchies ~ Elitists of Capitalism.
Vatican Invested Mussolini's blood money in a property portfolio!
Ponzi Scams rolled out as Holy proclamations at the High Altar.
Divinely 'In Debt We Trust' - hypnotizing of the full congregation.
Feeding frenzy of Hyper-Financial predators in the inner sanctum.
Reading out the Illusion, delusions spewing from the golden pulpit.
Speculative, Conglomerate, rapacious Cryptocrats, Priest craft.
There is no honest regulator offering scrutiny to this fornication
of being ripped off, by your own Government and justice system.
Where were the auditors on Wall St. protecting us from Rogues?
Rules that are working for the Banksters, corruption to their core.
No due diligence, Investing in greed patterns of Economic Crime.
Hedge fund, insurance, Real estate subprime mortgage gambling,
fraudulent lending practices, changing the interest rates at a whim!
Let's have another Plea bargaining, fines for all the biggest banks.
Developed $100 billion loans, designed to fail! Faith in Moloch.
Deception built into the bricks of your home, property bubbling.
Crisis of oversight giving political contributions to hide the blight.
"All the monies have been made, now shredding the evidence."
This is Racketeering on a Global scale and they are spinning it.
Democracy 'land of the Free' bending the law to suit themselves.
HSBC, Barclays, Standard Chartered and Wall Street's finest!!
Your Collateralised Number! Switched the Matrix from the Birth-
Certificate Fund! Controlling the whole population of your country.
Time to put in a new system of Love Programs into our Data bank.

*

It's all about empathy and all that thing

*They were looking at different molecules*in Invisible, empty Space.*
Exiled because they ate the apple of the Tree of knowledge. Why?
What about the ALL IN ONE? Kicked out for sinning never let back in!
Ego developing consciousness, creating dualities ~ over time falling.

Very Smacky

Projections ~ "I know Opium feels ok even when throwing up!"
Holding intent becoming reality * Cosmic convergence presence.
Pineal gland ~ right interface between consciousness & matter
"We're already a Space ship so why do we need another one?"
On one side to give it a push ~ the other It's just happening.
We identify ourselves by our thoughts ~ Vibrating Synthesis.
"What are you?" "I am Awake, living in the stillness"
"We have to own the power of Creation"

*

Inter Fear Ring * Maya

Need free space on all levels ~ healing within himself.
'Slaves to our own desires & aversions to pain'
You are not your Mind; Unplug Herr. Freund.
Free to think how we want ~ Out of control!
"Thinking leads to more thinking Professor"
Humans with a crisis of Consciousness ~
Come just be & enjoy * all we have to do.
Feel the soft Pinks of Unconditional Love

*

Manifestation in the Mayan Calendar

Long blonde hair, high heels, no pants, delicious, gorgeous ~
'They're not gonna come and stick a shotgun up your f.... arse!'
If you are movin' everything's easy; fixed, they put chains on you.
They have to realize whatever they've lived through laughing it up.
All happening through frequency ~ you'll fall in Unconditional love.
How could you possibly know who you are? Daddy where are we?
Having the luxury of time ~ flowing down the river.
"We're all innocent children in the soul of God"
Violet, silver ~ golden flames of purification.
She's a platinum blonde, Crystal from Minsk.
Zero is in the happening * Sat Chit Ananda

A Theme to Be Developed

And I would like to say that according to the Mayan Calendar ~
December 21st 2012 marks the end of the Macha and the beginning
of Pacha. It is the end of selfishness and the beginning of brotherhood.
It is the end of Individualism and the beginning of Collectivism.
Scientists know very well that this marks the end of a anthropocentric
life and the beginning of a Bio*centric life. It is the end of hatred and
the beginning of Love. The end of lies and the beginning of Truth.
It is the end of sadness and the beginning of joy.
It is the end of division and the beginning of Unity.

Evo Morales ~ President of Bolivia.
At UN General Assembly, 67th Session
*

Moslem rap, Hindu dub, Hasidic hiphop, Christian house, Zen electro

'Want another Pain Killer?' Industrialisation's War on Mother Nature!
'Extraordinary abduction' ~ tortured in every way over at Abu Gharaib!
Didn't know about Auschwitz cut the World knows of Guantanamo Bay.
No excuses, "Didn't you hear wailing at the bloody wall?" No hoaxes!
Breaking esoteric myths, Ciphers, False flags, Secret taboos' taboos!
Not money but lifestyle ~You can't know everything so surrender a bit
*

Knowing their Brutal Psyche

The Empire always wants to EXPAND ~ And Expand & ...
Which State has the largest Military Industrial Complex?
Keeping what you got & getting More & More - motivation.
Vast demands, less resources, states of unconsciousness!
For the Academically Educated, a Brainwashing Program?
Who's in charge of the Mind-Control Generator Inspector?
Switching on his Plasma Chi * Tesla's Singularity Toaster.
Pulling energy just in from the ethereal ~
Fresh air from an aero-dynamic waterfall.
Salmon flying ~ in this magical vibration

Directions to the Norms ~ Hang it on the bridge
'Given us a Global Elite Dictating, Making Problems then Offering
us the Solutions!' Oh yes we'll have some of that; In desperation!
Now they've taken over and they Own YOU! Nothing holistic here.
"Come and have some Cocaine?" ~ "I'm trying to get away from it!"
Spending his money and wasting his time! Why should I resist it!?
Why Am I here? You're here for a Party ~
A super friendly Psychedelic Space Picnic.

*

'Neti Neti' ~ Unlimited freedom of Vision
At The NEW REPUBLIC HOTEL ~ 'Less is more not less' mate.
'Madame Guillotine's Unplugged Global Tour 2012'. Choppy chop!
Dividing & Conquering AGAIN; They've alleged that Jesus was a ~.
*Our Totalitarian **Military I. C**; small elite Power had something to say*
On the 'Domination Program!' "Who's Stolen all the Global Wealth?"
The World is run by criminal gangs; We are crack Zombies of sorts!
They never wanna empower the people ~ Can't predict next instant.
'Democratic Dictatorship' ~ Read the Secrets of the Rich & Powerful
Erasing the tape of Y/our Minds ~ cleansing mass unconsciousness.
Where did you get your perceptions * understanding of self ~ nature?
Discard it all, polarity, propaganda, conditionings; 'Not this ~ Not this'
* All One substance ~ Realizing everything is Cosmic Consciousness.
What's goin' through your brain? Livin' Oblivion in apparent duality ~
Why the need to always put a Meaning and not go with the flow?
Who eats holism? Simple hedgehogs can't swim!

*

Mr Lustre * Cum Laude!
'Voyaging through the Mind' ~
She's running on Purest Cosmic Love.
On a full tank, soaking her flood plains!
"I'll hold you" "I'll hold you Inside me."
"Was that a glorious fuck?" Making Love ~
That was Love fully together in the moment.

Bio*Cellular

How would you define a lipstick? Wanted to display her beauty.
Looking in a tin mirror, reflection ~ shining amongst all that poverty.
Distracted by Image, I want some of that! The Rolls Royce of Acid.
'The Uppers, downers, sleepers, leapers, Dexies, Purple Hearts!
Blind man tasered by Police, 'we apologise for any inconvenience'
Desperate Alice going down a rabbit hole, "eat me, drink me etc….
& people from humble backgrounds who become magically rich!
Singaporean Robotic trees, I'm more for the feelin' than meanin'
"I don't care I live in Goa, let the World go on its own course!"
What can I do I'm just spreadin' my love

*

Pagan Fayre ~ Street Festival ~ Mercurial Village

I've got my idea but that makes sense too, ask Mr. Jimi Hendrix.
It's more in the creativity than the Egoism, like a rocket crossing
the Universe of the Mind ~ carrying Cosmic evolution inside you.
Not many rebels left ~ just to let you know who's the boss!
No they're not the Boss! Something natural's happening.
In Tune going for it ~ with it, energy; Just letting it be free.

*

She Shone in Rubies & Sapphires

'A lion's roar can be heard for over 5 kms. in the wild' "GRRRH!"
Google will give you the answer as to which corner you light up.
Went purely vertical out Zoomed him and shot his wing in flames.
His German relative said she had died in the 'Eugenics Program'
Sad they hit a landmine; Everyone has a breaking point General!

*

Mr. Badger's Trauma

He said, "Elephants what good are they?" "A big mistake ~
"You broke my heart the moment I laid eyes upon your eyes"
'It's a reflection of the Connection' Shit hot; Smiling assassins!
"Enjoy your moment ~ without me"

Where is our Saviour?
No military importance blown to smithereens, collateral damage!
Just another brutal horrendous massacre see it every day on TV.
How about Y/our human instincts? Who is realising these facts?
Living with No Hope and Full of Fear, believing it, is killing us!
Another visionary trip or delusionary propaganda of the Chaos.
No salvation for those arriving on another unromantic Slave Ship!
She exists on the edge of Hades, full out of Control, chained spirits.
Escaped its bedlam for nights out at the Coliseum crack cat house!
Death of a young Satyr ~ his emotions spread all over the ground.
No time to frolic, just been given a golden light cellular healing.
Erotic investigation of thoughts ~ Enhancing poetic imagination.
Mellow Drama * Mellow Prana

*

In the End!
They love it the slaves, watching the Tsar, the Queen, those with
lots of diamonds on; Palace waltzing, you're frozen in a Tin mine!
"Go in the name of God & St George & make havoc on the poor!"
Is there absolutely no empathy in the hearts of the Plutocracy?
A Tyrant's Cossacks Murdering his own people!
"What if the bleeding doesn't stop?"
Megalomaniac couple at the Top.
Hyper Paranoid about their Sins.
They're all gonna get shot….
Wielding Autocratic Power
Another fuckin' Massacre!

*

Terror & Control Your Highness
Feeling naked without his briefcase, carrying the nuclear codes.
Okhrana spies on every step; "Shut Parliament, I AM The Tsar!"
Who do you believe in Caesar? Where is the divine spirit living?
'Informers everywhere no one trusts anyone' ~ All for the Power!

Natural Connection
Love of mystery, contact between genitalia of sensuality & You!
Gaining a woman's heart ~ Kama swimming in her eyes of desire.
Satisfying ourselves through our extraordinary six human senses.
Being in sublime touch*Consciousness of Cupid's arising pleasure.
'She'll never disregard a man kneeling at her feet.'
Embrace her according to how she likes it.
Just being yourself ~ that Instant is Alive
*

Summer Afternoon
What's on the Master's Mind with Cruise Missiles flying about?
Troops in full Riot gear tasering, pepper spraying the Citizenry!
How did this begin, who set it up, why and how's it gonna end?
Infinite examples of Man's crazy, cruel in/actions on innocents.
Do you really want this in your Life and that of your children?
'Live the Life you want to see in the World'
*

Rainbow Butterfly #16
Her mouth aching ~ aching with desire and wet revelation!
Who has the key to her scented, rampant, sublime garden?
Sex loaded with Psychic Taboos ~ Surreality on the attack!
Breaking all the stereotypes ~ Liberations of Your Mind.
Change the identity, expectation, definition, judgment ~
Seeing realism from different, amazing, fresh perceptions.
Provocative, extravagant, dreamer becoming LSD King.
Taking ordinary concepts and feeling Cosmic energy ~
The Self, Idols, great sacred cows, myths of our culture.
Theatre for the memories of the Mind ~ No Mind Space.
Multi orgasms transcending the fabric of Illusion.
Let's have some Dionysian super ecstasy together.
Got to be in the moment * subconscious climaxes.
Rescued sweet Innocence ~ laid her at my feet.
We're part of creating a beautiful New World

Dancing in the shoes of time
You got the life in the cupboard… No way!!
The 'Sacred JOB' ~ It's the Acquiescent Slave!
He's an economic drone, working for the Man from Babylon!
"The guy who read her cards sort of cracked up and cried!"
Ended by just doing it ~ putting the brainwashing in the bin.
My friend gave two upset Grey parrots Psychic healings.

*

Alliances
Married for family, for money for position; Like our Royalty!
"We have a Love Marriage but my husband's family exiled us"
Chose a different path to the norm ~ That took courage!
The fact is that the family don't wanna hear about 'LOVE'
Jumped out the box and you can't go back in it the same ~
Psyches of India, Bangkok, another harem, the Suite of Slaves!
'Love' ~ Not to be with your feelings is a contradiction in Space.
"Where is the Love then? Yeah where is the Love man?"
They're not wrapped up in all the emotion

*

*L S D * Travels*
Smack the rat, hit the bell and get the croc of gold!
You've got it ~ but it's not to be; a hard Drive Defrag.
She was a barmaid on the Banana Plantation, Livin' in.
Met City boy from the checkered square Inner Sanctum!
It's so simple and it's in us ~ all we gotta do is Tap it!
Yes it excited her, her choice… to Enjoy.
If it makes your heart sing ~ It's for You.
Stay with that, work with that, enjoy with that; All an Inside job
You either enjoy it or you don't ~ to be or not to be UN/HAPPY.
If you feel that we have to put our foot down on the brake ~
then we go into a skid, try to Control it ~ monkey mind ambush!
"He's havin' pleasure in tellin' me how little I was gonna receive!"
"You wouldn't get bail if you were in a steel drum band!"

Natur * Laterally

Configuring ~ no straight lines in the Cathedral of Sig. Gaudi!
Standing outside the Grand Duomo of illusion and confusion.
In psychedelical wonder, inspirationally, marvelous splendor.
Don't need the shame, guilt, resentment, blame, name, game.
'These are your feelings, sensations, be equanimously aware'
Accept effortlessly, Rejoice, empowered in the unconditioned ~
Not Electric shock therapy, she brought him fresh, juicy ecstasy.
He relished the unexpected*excitement of sweet Rosie's gelati.
Opening up windows onto hallucinogenic meadows of delight.
Aurora Borealis' explosions in an elemental, iridium night sky

*

"He's eaten a big hash muffin"

Missed the sunset ~ that's being stoned!
"I asked them not to bite me and they got the message"
Coke ~ "You know what to do when you're in Brazil then!"
Where's the Guarana? "What the fuck is happening ~ you wonder"
If you gotta drive out bad spirits, they'd use Torture, Fire & a Rack!
'There are no walls that separate us except those we make ourselves,
in our own Minds' ~ See Miro's ~ 'la Poetess' la beautiful Seductress.
It's not Catatonic Platonic, Devil may care or taking too many liberties

*

An Array of Despots

Riding through the desert on a horse with RFI Tags ~ Abnormal!
Why does the human brain continue to let this destruction exist?
Electrons are dancing throughout zero point energetic fields ~
Bring me Aphorisms, Sutras, Koans, Qurans, Delphic maxims,
Inscribed on the exquisite golden vases of Pythagorean muses.
"I Love you." ~ "You got a funny way of showing it" sonnets.
'Erase your minds and put in what?' Expectations overrider!
Bringing new courtesans from the Pink Nymphaeum.
Gave up their egos to a Neo pagan from Eros' moon.
"What beautiful space"

Ayhuascan Huipiles

Magic play ~ you see the weaving rainbows.
Bringing it in the action makes it believable.
Free will ~ Use it or forever lose it.
Rubik cubes, a big puzzle, Kaleidoscopic 360* pictures.
No more angles to hide, no more fractions of the whole.
Going into the 5th dimension ~ we get another sunbeam.
Dreamy Weddings over happy crystallite energies

*

"There Is No Spoon"

A piece of a Jigsaw ~ filling in the empty hole of space.
Proper Communication ~ helps us see the Whole puzzle.
Sharing evolution ~ not taking all the Good things for granted!
There's hallucinations everywhere interacting with neurons in
your static brain. 'The Truth Is there Is No Truth' ~ 'Neti Neti'
Do your best (in being) in the moment ~ of eternity.
How do you want your Mind to sing ~ for humanity,
Yeah, how do you want ~ your heart to sing?
What did you get living out in Mystical Tibet?
It's all in your head * Milky Way's everywhere.
'Truth Is Truth' ~ Where it takes your Spirit

*

You'll never know now

You can't kill every Daisy like you can't kill every fly or mosquito ~
What's the point, another one only comes back and then another!
Why mow the grass? The point is the lawn's supposed to be green!
A Public Nuisance, "I wanna throw a brick through a Bank window"
"They destroyed every positive emotion" Try a drink called FUN.
I love listening to the workings of your brain; "Any old, any old iron?"
Contemplating Erato's love poetry ~ amusing the daughters of Zeus.
Sprinkling us with baby fairy dust; Alive with spirits ~ sacred Muses.
Short and sweet ~ Keep those Golden prayer flags spinning high

Fantastic & Beautiful ~ Rich golden threads
Visual wonder & sensual expression, this is the poetry I love,
which takes Us on a magical mystery tour of the Universe ~
in your heart, this is Inspiration to empower your lover to walk
hand in hand with you through the burning white hot Cosmic fires
of nature and to melt me in her Yoni furnace into love alchemy.
Your words are sublime, Astral ~ ethereal, demure, subtley serene.
Your references are the beginning of a new style of Cosmic erotology
which was painted on the bejeweled walls of exotic Tantric Temples.
Laughter in the seraglios of Princes ~ You have captured its essence,
drinking at the pure fountain of a Goddess, tasting her sweet nectar's
wet spot, you are sharing the sacred dripping ambrosia, you are ~
feeling divine, you are channeling Venus' fragrant perfumed bliss.
I'm in a Pleasure garden of delight with you, buds of anticipation
are bursting inside me as the full Moon is lighting heaven's night!

*

The Inhumanity of 'Legal' Personnel Land Mines!
"In the course of your duty you may have the luck to run into
contact with the enemy, the Anti Christ; Kill everyone of them fuckers!"
'Now is the time to perfect a total war economy' Mr. Global Financier.
Controlling of all Technologies +/- ~ Why have you got Illegal weapons,
Murdering Magnums, Killing Drones, A Bombs, Kali's Transmutation?
Who sold them illegal Thermite Explosives? Justice for All coming in!
The Advisers of the Advisers in that game of Fake Snake oil, Sheik.
"They need to be in a Maximum Prison lock-up down in the swamps"
Individualized Perception of a supremacist God is the American dream

*

Poisoning Relations
All the extended cousins turned out on the balcony for the fly past!
"People dressed up from the Job Centre Not a real Roman Legion!"
Same time Aung San Suu Kyi is accepting her Nobel Peace Prize.
A Soul Prisoner under house arrest; took her 15 years to get here!
Sharing her experience ~ enlightening discourse on Human Rights

Extremely Censored

Who's protecting Bradley Manning's 1st Amendment of Free speech?
'Centaurs erect with a large Trident pointing it at Lucifer's Evil eye'
K VISUALS ~ "I couldn't fall off the floor, I just sat there…!"
"You know you're not sheeple in a stupor, you're a shepherd!"
No sheep in India, full of harpsichords; so many stupid people take
themselves too seriously, your Auto-immune system's Reactions!
Have you got to meditate to be Buddhist? Don't cost anything?
The myth of Psycho analysis ~Then he found himself!

*

Open Mind at the Pleasure Palace

"I'm actually doing it; you think you can do it, Fuck off!"
Voice over ~ Realization of the Prison your mind can be in!"
You wouldn't get a fuck out of me if I was reading a good book.
Fucked up Mentality I don't wanna know their silly prejudices…
No time to make Love, too busy making her deadline!
For fuck sake calm down, shut up and choose a place.

*

'No fish in the Pool'

Showing Freedom can and does exist ~ surfing through taboos
Show yourself in your whole character, throw out all dualities
into the World, interacting with Jupiter shining from in me ~
at that instant where Sun & Moon are in Cosmic alignment.
Leveling all Limitation ~ Go, that's our sense of Liberation.
Right now ~ all packed; "Might be going up in a flying saucer"
"Bye bye, gave her my jewelry and the car; She Understood."
Can go at anytime ~ everything is possible in this Crystal net.
Direct openings to the Gateway **'The Intent is in the Reality'**
Hooked on that gorgeous girl but looking for the vital Point.
We are Conscious ~ Now we are waking up to it.
A softer allowance giving us the Space to be in it.
Tantric sexuality steaming through the frequency
Let's all share in some absolute Love

Creative Art ~ lets your Imagination run #1
Abstract*logic operational System ~ being less creative
is more left side of brain ~ Instincts from your right side!
Encouraging the inner river ~ magical Indigo children alive.
Let's be more connected to multi ~ Synchronicity Serendipity...
Formulae following Patterns and Programs means more Controls.
With Imagination you don't know what's coming next. The Unknown,
flowing instantly ~ no predetermined expectation of how it is to be.
Surreal what is Really Real Reality? Esoteric is Realism here*now.
Streaming sub Consciousness ~ Mind is flowing in No Mind Space.
No Time or place ~ No distractions, delusions or extra dualities
over mass conditioned Identity ~ in this moment is the moment

*
Anything Non Abstract is of 'Something' ~ some 'FORM' Shape.
Something Accepted by Mass consciousness' ~ Mind as 'Real'
No naked pubic, pearlescent women waiting for a Tram at night.
Abstract is empty silence, there's no house, no woman, no horse,
no fishing boat on a big wave, no walk in duality's summer's park,
no Haystack, no cobbled street in a snowy winter's cottage village.
No chapeau melon, no Pipe. no Narcissus' reflection in a mirrored,
pool of iridescence, no cubist breasts, no Italian futurist in the frame

*
Recording a concept, projection, perception, chemical connection,
holographic brain ~ in which hemisphere is your 'ID' wandering?
Instantaneous Digital Photonic Manifestation, Intent from where?
Including your own interpretation of emotions ~ synapse reaction.
Sultry females staring at a Green fairy from the Galaxy of Botany.
So much time to unravel in our own deluded, subjective Mindset.
It's not a paranoid, dissociated illusion, embrace it as the Theatre.
Feeding the programs with our thoughts ~ realizations of a vision.
Mixing the colors of luminosity into your own unknown open space

Classical Abstraction #2
They're recognizable, reconfigured, materialized, constructs ~
In the 3rd dimensional with planes, colours, textures, geometry,
upside down brush strokes, Cubism, impressionism, donkeys in
the sky flying over church spires, bird's nests, incubating eggs.
'Expressionism' ~ any new techniques to make the product Real.
Just let it go ~ flow, Open Mind IS Space, open heart, open conscious
that is truly Original ~ unique, from your own Individualistic reflections.
"Don't tell me Mona Lisa didn't take her clothes off lad?"
*

Salon des Abstractions et L'Imagination
Touching something 'Real' being accepted by the same values!
Not looking for New, Alien, indefinable to exhibit on your walls.
Happy enough to hang a picture from IKEA as an Image of Art.
How much was that worth in the market of Guns and butter?
Made a serigraph of Jackie O, Mao Zedong, Elvis Presley, Che
Guevara, Andy Warhol touches a subconscious ~ synergy nerve.
Synchronicities ~ are butterflies fluttering around Artists' studios.
What's your Motivation, modulation ~ Success and who told you?
Better to make Love not War ~ let Control go and Allow FREELY.
And change the program about the Cossacks beating up the Jews!
*

True Creativity is Allowed to flow from where?
*Experimenting, experiencing Source ~ essence of Space*Mind.*
Breaking all the Moulds, whatever they may be and from whom?
Creativity is more than a great painting hanging in time & space
and certified by the Authorities, by the bureau des Psychopeuts.
"Unfortunately these Wonders from Polynesia do not Conform to
our convention, to what we have determined is correct Art." Yet
we haven't even realized that the Imagination is the magic fairy,
the Subconscious' fountain of indefinable Cosmic Abstraction.

Uncensored Space Energy #3

Because you didn't have to sell it for any reason, for money!
Manifesting what You feel, Your Intention*Subconsciously ~
Realizations of the choices made and given to us by whom?
Which source do you hear ~ the silence, nature, the Empire?
Which catalyst, Psychedelia, DNA; Karma, heart, mind, Space?
"You don't need to wear your flip flops walking on the beach ~
out of Touch with nature, which is what you don't want to be!"

*

Trials & Tribulations ~ In the Bin

'Vue du Chateau d'eau et le Palais de l'Electricite'
Passed a mirror vendor hawking at a Peruvian landing strip.
Public Servants have taken on the role to serve the Public ~
not us the public serving them and undermined by corruption &
GREED because they have assumed ~ POWER gives them the
Right to be Tyrants & Dictators, justified by their laws and priests.
What is so different from when Jesus stood there condemned?
Defunct - do you enjoy having humans enslaved to Fuck with?
How do you look them in the eye and have lucid dreaming?
Hallucinations, dramas, nervous disorders, all in your DNA.
More Distractions & Delusions, obsessed puppets in command!
'Life is simple ~ Sharing Loving Kindness, from the Heart'
She touched something real in her*self* same as being here now.
Respect ~ had a Revelation from having a Love Affair with you.
Serving us to find the meaning of Life not kept in the F... dark!
More Fun and games from the Holy Grail, not a Moneyfesto.

*

The War Happened!

'His poetry has the emotional resonance of Classical Masters.
Who believed Art could change the World ~ or even a human?'
Let's portray reality as it pertains to the consequences of poverty,
human tragedy, your destiny expressed in a Sutra of Serendipity

S L A V E B R O K E R #9

Fight for your chapatti and tell her to Fuck Off! Can't do that.
At least You can look yourself in the face and carry on!
Battering each other's brains in a fight to the DEATH!
He Owns Him ~ How many Slaves do you Possess?
And what's her name? She's Bewilder, an Afro American Alien.
Coded Receipt; She's black, female, Slave from another Continent!
From a jungle village, across rivers, mountains, valleys, Oceans!
What happened to all yur own Indian tribes and sacred Buffalo?
Unburdened by DNA. floating in your genes from out of Delirium.
She is my Sole Private Property; I have a correct bill of sale!
"She's Your Slave Mr!" ~ 'LIBERIAN BLACK SALE'
All the finest Specimens to do with whatever you so desire.
"What will you have me do Master?" Whipped her black ass!
Genocidal charade on parade

*

Feeling Invisible Space

Click! "It's good to move on ~
It's not even stopping the mind....
more like Living the moment of eternity ~
not going down the same path for six years!
My reaction to it, freely accepting it for what it is.
Finally rewiring my whole crystal network
couldn't cope with my perceived 'reality'
Why let something upset you again?
Just that little beam of light I needed
to convert it ~ the World is as it is.
I will never be unhappy and which point
of view do you take to understand that?
You make Thoughts ~ in this room
where my head was so full of shit!
Transition from undergrowth Turmoil.
Understanding the World ~ of my Life

IMPLANTED

"Tell them in the kitchen to make less of a racket!"
The Rich don't Need this Work embedded Program.
Out of this System as they can afford to be … Free!
He has the chance to be out and live a simpler life but
he doesn't want it. Needs the money, security, Identity!
Some have a nice life but committed to the JOB or fired!
Don't fancy the FEAR of the Unknown mate; a big Taboo.
Resistance to any change ~ something New from the brain,
left side needs rational, logic, order for it to function correctly
under the direction of dualities, educated values, national bias.
Who told you to do that, who's your Commanding Officer mate?
The whole realm of your understanding, consciousness is SET;
Unusual deviations will be appropriately and strongly dealt with!
Never got round to thinking if my Imagination had any Realness.
Oh he's a crazy artist, gifted musician, mad intelligent person but
where did it come from and why am I a character in outer space?
I am such and such a Model in this Anthropologic Rubik cubensis.
What is Original, the essence, who Am I, my Spirit, is it Illusion,
upon illusion, a labyrinth of Egos, 1984 dystopia, a holier book,
direction to a paradise by way of a Semtex abomination on You?
What is desire, what is Love; Am I just a widget paying VATaxes
to a hierarchy of Superior Souls? No * & You are Cosmic energy.

*

Invalid Care

"You're supposed to come over here to cheer me up ~ from Grief!"
"I dunno what's up with you and he's havin' a nice game of golf!"
Need clear light to reach the coral * box jellyfish have 24 eyes!
Who's polluting Seagrass meadows? All depending on visuality
Interdependent habitats ~ Your mother is painfully dying in HD!
Sustain natural harmony, Great Barrier reefs of supernatural Clarity.
Google it, see 'Reefs in terminal decline' ~ from a satellite in Space.

They Killed the Power
Not a drop of blood was wasted at a Public execution!
Groomed to be in the Royal household. "Bend over ~"
Threw out the Tyrant, waiting for the next one to arrive!
The Rule of subjects ~ excluding all women and slaves.
Creating confidence in her so she may grow to Love him.
There's letting go of all worldly distractions ~ turning inward.
Don't need another foreign Invasion, this is my Temple!
Free ~ to be Spiritual, to have Inner Peace.
Water is connecting the emotional ~
*

Satyagraha Trench
Shouted to subvert, rebel with Soul Force, use your power to
transform not convert. The Machine knows best is its slogan.
What about spontaneity ~ fateful destiny, gravity, serendipity?
How about disordering structures, models for paradigm shifts?
Attuning to the true ireality needs a revolution of Love Magic.
Essential, irrational, right side polarity of no dualistic dynamos.
Throw all those logical nincompoops, turds into the silicon bath.
Worldly Mind pattern of Power and control over other usurpers.
Terrified to let go, you conscript us into your schizophrenia.
"Forward lads over the barricades, under the wire; FIRE!!"
*

Intolerable
Mental Illness of epidemic proportions in the World's populous ~
Images not censored by the conditioned mind to categorise away.
Let's have an unofficial, unsanctified pagan love affair my beauty.
Let's Open up an Unconscious Mind to find magical cheesecakes.
Primitively inspired geometry in metamorphic, surreal landscapes
of human erotic, passionate, beautiful, cruel, magnificent, MIND.
Let it go on a safari into the wilderness face to face with a Tigress,
feeling sensations of sacred communion with the naturally divine.
These are Your fears inside You (OWN IT!) becoming self aware

The Point

Is right we still got SLAVE written on our back!
The only difference is that it's in glittering Bling.
Super slick, super slinky cocaine, sturdy birds.
Shouting at the Tele, sitting with baited breath!
Come give me, give me, give me, tell me, tell me.
Don't give me that bollocks, listen it's all bollocks!
Deep in you fear, deep in you distraction is how much generosity?
Emotionally challenged ~ Stay in the LOVE VIBRATION matey!
Reflecting when you're not swimming in the Love pool.
Things come up, the journey of Self-discovery is now.
Amazement for me; It's Amazing because it's Amazing!
Don't talk to me about bollocks!
"I Love talkin' Life UP & UP"

*

'Shanti Shanti' ~ Let's See It!

Get out the way, you know what I mean ~
Goin' out of the Mind ~ without going mad.
This Parallel Universe, you've slipped in to….
And you paid the money, you've paid yu ticket.
Gone yourself in and had the experience ~
Isn't that what tripping's all about?
We're Not here to sit in Judgment.
Going through the motion ~ getting that bit of freedom.
Trimming the bush of a small crack on a smooth, wet wall.
Off the top of me head, Yeah you got the way and let it rip!
That's on my Shield, You cannot take me down.
Clearing of the past ~ the residue of that, his story.
I used to go and fill up my cup with human kindness.
Everything you thought it should be and there you go!
Breaking Free! Needed a breakdown of my Nervous System.
"I'm Happy with my Life" ~ Living one's own Invincible Truth.
'This Truth Will Set You Free'

Being the Pendulum
I do believe in trying not to react, don't fan the energy ablaze.
"I remember my happy, dippy, hippy friends
who could be as forgetful as a fluffy cloud"
Ego, control get out the way ~ let the free
flow come
*
-

You're a Fecund Love Jewel
"If it's got eyes it's not vegetarian!"
"I'll be there because I wanna be there,
if I don't wanna be there, I won't be there"
No words just the beat ~ Sharing the Pleasure.
Inhaling, want re-erection, new reflection not election.
Appreciating a slow ejaculation, you can cum all over me!
So endowed, strong, cherished in her deeply, snug fit pussy.
Exciting scents ~ impregnated with the perfume of aphrodisiacs
gaining control; Her buttocks' possession of my power to reason.
The sight is ravishing from behind ~ I knew she wanted shagging.
It's in this virile moment!
*

Vision 11
*Being ~ being * Om Passion Om * Om Wonder Om* Om Beauty Om**
Om Peace Om * Om Bliss Om * Om Love Om * BOm * Omni * Om
The Illusion of Separation ~ we create in our Minds.
If you say anything is 'this object' you create duality ~
Impermanence, so don't be Attached to it ~ LETTING GO
No one knows Jack Shit really ~ it's all a massive delusion
about conceptualizing, Judgments, names, Identities, polarities.
*I Think therefore I AM*Separated I ~ Constructing it in 'My MIND.'*
Seems to be Insane Mental Conditioning, Karma and all that stuff!
Every moment is an opportunity to be Conscious in Life of Space.
What are we doing with the Opportunity? Basically Here I AM ~
No separation ~ if you can accept it's all a big mind distraction!

Too much Toxicity!

'100 cacao beans bought an Aztec a slave,12 for a courtesan'
What is in the eye of your mind? He's lost his grip on reality!
'Some kind of Revolutionary ~ wrestling with my conscience.
Damn them all!' This is our Holy range of Sacrificial gowns...
What's happened to being Innocent until proven to be guilty?
Exaggerating the Ideological war on a bloody chopping block.
Exaggerating cultural, gender divides, dropped a 5 ton concrete
block on her head for their adultery; Forbidden to throw stones!
"I think I'm in Love" ~ I don't want any misunderstanding & pain

*

Economy Tanked!

The man at the Top > Who lives, who dies, who is put in chains?
Going to War as the most powerful, righteous, national Identity.
$350 million a day in Afghanistan ~ Bombing rocks & civilians!
Immolation still common, barbaric practices on innocent women.
Found wreckage of a British Slaver ~ all were thrown overboard.
Distant ghostly figures on the shore ~ seeping into a misty ocean.
How about that, a tyrannical Mindscape, officially legalized murder!
SLAVERY is thriving ~ What is the Genesis for a human rebellion?

*

Thorn * Apples

Excited by the approaching prospect of a sweet fuck with you!
Gathering his energy from deep down ~ dreams of sunflowers.
New perspective giving us a new expressive, visual language.
Feeling life as a gift without your sanctimonious religion ~
Painting what she has in her heart ~ Cosmic Rays cuming.
STOP Invading my Privacy as if it had no meaning at all!
Why not invest in the cultivation of biodiversity, focus on nature.
Nothing more delightful ~ man & woman, burning in Love's glow.
Flower child, Love child, Sunshine child switched on to amorous.
Nails scratching her breasts, driven by unquenched fury

Gold Taps & Existential Klitty Cats
Later she married a follower of the Stratocaster Prophet.
They were more committed then, they still had the Spirit.
"I recognized him from the playpen at my friend's brothel"
Banged to rights! Hammering of the Gods!
They don't give a fuck man! Shimmering late ~
Coming through the black holes ~ All the things we are.
Penny whistles, Gaelic harmonies just around the corner ~

*

What's Your Name?
Khush Trance Baba's got the spirit of ten ~ hopping semen!
Oh I Love your eyes, charming with no intention to disguise…
Getting to learn what they need to know; We're in heaven here,
just to know there's a hell existing ten minutes down the road!
Let's make a new garden of Eden in the Primavera air waves.
We can make things to take us round the Solar system
but people still behaving like Neanderthals ~ Mutilation
cutting the clitoris out of a young girl to make her pure!
Imposed their barbaric will on your innocent daughters.
Don't stone her because she's wearing Victoria's secret.
Influencing the traditions ~ Systems to change the Warring.
People don't know it, tell the Truth it's not in the main media.
Emigrated to an island ~ Reading between all the lines.
Swimming across the channel in an unofficial Burka.
If she wants to wear an invisible bikini ~ 'Inshallah'
Casting her out onto the Razor wire!

*

Sweet Tawaf * Is it about Empowering me? OK!
Kissing the black vulva of the Goddess ~ Objective of ritual ecstasy!
All*lat worshipping at her pagan cubist shrine ~ in bright Sunshine.
'Directed Energy Weapons' not the humiliation of gettin' busted!
"Admitted, Jordan used torture but not as much as they used to"

'Collateral Murder'

Post anti-fascism war ~ dire Poverty swept onto Venetian shores.
Who's against the abuse of Power, challenging Official Diktats?
Accepted belief that the media is working for the public good?
Accepted belief that Government is working for the public good.
Accepted belief that business is regulated for the public good.
Absolutely untrue, it's fake, it's ALL corrupt, deadly, false view.
Psychological warfare from Y/our cradle to grave manipulation.
Breaking down totalitarian manias for one dimensional meaning.
Be truly creative, interdependent, multi dimensional perspectives.
'Appearance' & 'Neo Realism' ~ Life keeps changing & so do we.
Beyond words, expressing this nature ~ human*omni*biodiversity

*

All the Composition of Atomised Grass

Opening to Spiritual Trance, sexual magic, orgasms of ecstasy.
Suffocating from the factories' fumes, she's become a neurotic!
"They want Meaning, not allowing a basis of uncertainties of life"
Let's have some Sensitivity to other aspects of Planetary living.
Beautiful visuals, abstract designs of exotic insects and flowers.
Looking into a non linear narrative between unspoken SPACES.
Impossible to analyze the 'Purposes' in the life of a bumble bee.
No ultimate Control Centre, be spontaneous ~ as it's happening.
'Seeing their emotional psychological responses in this moment'

*

Allow it to happen*Pagan Priapus' Cock's*Energetic Magnetism

Curiosity Not Aggression ~ I'm a tourist in a transparent bubble.
It's all there to TEMPT YOU, an exotic, erotic nature Angelette.
Universal Laws of Attraction; Intention to have some of that Eros.
& I want a Super yacht with a supermodel crew from les Antilles.
Manifesting what you want; What are you contributing Maestro?
'My thoughts combined with emotions ~ vibrating out from you
(here & now/time & space) throughout the Cosmos'

Pious Phallus!

Wakes up with a sexy chick fanning him ~ Romantic Maya!
Falling into the Love Pool ~ Lost in tribal bliss,
living alone in one's manifested Golden Light.
Who's forgotten about bringing Krishna's water?
"I am the underlying all" ~ Dimensional changes.
Fell into his own dream*he kept the Divine waiting!
Like walking into a Hologram ~ but this one is real!
"Shiva is Bhagwan's ego" ~ Big Cosmic Space in us.
"What's the last thought leaving your body gorgeous?"
Concentration between the brows ~ going straight up, out!
'And then Krishna took him for a walk in the forest....!'

*

Bhakti ~ Sufi

Just dancing like a Madman, his Mind only on God ~
out for Peace, Love, Freedom ~ Transcendental Nataraj.
Waking up your Serpent ~ might see String Theory for Real!
Very Intense the Earth's vibrating waves ~ The Full Trip.
"Maya is there to strengthen your Love of the Divine ~"
"Not all progress is moving forward ~ in a plastic Ocean"

*

Frangipani Preference

You are a shiny Star ~ Golden frequency.......
Knowing that you can go out of your Mind and come back fine.
"I always had the Impression he would become a crazy lunatic!"
Ebbing, flowing of the real Cosmic Ocean ~ Transcendentalism.
"It's so random, doesn't feel like you're in any subliminal Program!"
It even contains apparent sounds and smells of the seaweed ~
Sweet sticky, perfume slowly oozing from a great Banyan tree.
Visions of Galactic Obelisks by a shimmering lake ~ Spiritually.
Your touch and kisses ~ torrents of warm nectar on my fingers.
Feeling Life ~ dripping Honey!

Six Senses

Entheogenic molecules * intermingling in a prism of vibrations ~
Bag of boiled eggs & bottle of poppers, switches on his Merkaba.
Depends on how much of my Allowance ~ Crusty, crunchy, tasty
Maggots, a new Addiction; "We are the Universal image of Itself."
Welcoming us ~ "The Gates are all Open, it's just our realisation"
All in one means all the same, even the evilest one in the World;
Needs more loving! "I bow down to kiss Gaia through compassion
and mercy & remember that I Am. An ID Chip in your number plate!
You go into colour's frequencies letting go of a concept of Your*self.
'Namaste, All in One, In Lak'ech, Inshallah, Amen; It's done'
"You were just a nanobot machine ~ No more soul frequency!"
Be in the stillness of the Zero ~ in the Oneness.
'Chapora girls sucking Big chillums!'
"That's all yu need, a lot more bliss"
She's dancing ~ it's her birthday.
*

Vertigoing

Jumping 110 floors in 10 seconds, what a choice in an Inferno!
Hey, to some they were on their way to Hell ~ committing a Sin
Unforgivable by God! 'Actions of others caused them all to die.'
Suicide not a fate of God these deaths were ruled as Homicide.
'All 2753 Official Victims died from their blunt Impact Injuries!'
1000+ still have yet to be identified from being Vapourised.
"The woman didn't scream as she fell past me."
Photos of 104 jumpers maybe 200 +, it must have felt like flying.
Falling 1350 feet out of a hole that an unexpected plane made!
Raining bodies ~ coming out of the sky like rockets!
After she hit the ground there was nothing left ~
'Falling Man' ~ no jumpers have ever been Officially Identified.
Did find fragments of bone, knew it was a loved one from DNA.
Real Naked terror.

Alluring Raw Clitolatte

Yin(*)Yang *Mind full *Mind less ~ being CLEAR ~ reflections,
Cosmic Heart, chakras, space, energy, vibration ~ frequency.
"She's not going to fuckin' shag someone in a tent is she?"
A couple o' pints, a fuck, a meat pie and a curry kebab…
My own Blow Job Queen ~ "Loyal 'til I find someone else!"
Enjoying first quality women; thus ends the Love quarrels.
Sensuous feelings' radiance vibrating beyond the Milky Way.
Cosmic passion celebrating our happiness * being together.
Stirring erotic hot magma juice ~ Reflecting Climaxing Inside
Irresistible Apsaras feasting in a Moon's brightly lit glade.

*

Duality * Kisser!

"Is the cage shut?" "Is the Bunker bolted?"
The soft side of Adolf ~ "He was a Pop star!"
'Don't mean a thing if it don't have that swing'
just whistlin' the melody of a Benny Goodman.
'Swing Heil'. Underground with the White Roses.
On My trip ~ She's riding with Full fear, FEAR!
Pulled over for lying in the grass full of crystals

*

Unnatural Selections

It's so random, doesn't taste like any kind of Program!
Looking out for what exactly? Shimmering solar lights….
I'm meditating on a sun bed, briefcase for my sandwiches.
Ebbing and flowing of the Real waves ~ of Cosmic Oceans.
The sounds and the smells of a jade green sea.
Perfumed air of frangipani ~ on a vanilla breeze
Feeling the spirituality of the Great Banyan trees.
Visions of Galactic Obelisks beside a dazzling lake.
Your touch, a kiss, a torrent of warm nectar on my fingers.
Feeling life ~ from in you

Unrequited Adoration ~ 't's Not that's your Wanting!
Transmigration is not like a balloon ~ floating from life to life.
Mindful ~ Mindless in a Theatre of Illusion, dreaming it all up.
"All Afraid of being Hooked on something ~ their ego's caught,
they don't want to have any Identification with anyone, anymore.
Running away from themselves only want a laugh and to be funky!
She can't hold the Focus on something she'd need to go too deep,
she'd then have to Reflect ~ not getting for herself all that Attention!
"Dumped she can't hold it up ~ for sure it's a Freedom" Outrageously!
Two sentences then she had to run away ~ It's Banana bullshit.
You don't even want to Identify with them… they're addicted.
In a drug fuelled loving relationship, our K. hole Connection!
Blanking out ~ harder to keep in a commitment, a relationship.
Is any Quality there, to Live it, to experience it? You miss out
your possibility of going deeper ~ living in an MDMA love trap.
Don't want to go in deep INTIMACY ~ Where do you want to go?
A stone is beautiful too ~ not only responding to the Superficial.
You are All what you give Yourself. Just wanting to be a Good
Human, is it being naïve, is she being too friendly as a hot chick?
Lighting Straw fires, big intense flames, burnt down very quickly!
Sucking up everything, Jump on; "She didn't promise anything!"
'Making friends now ~ as it is, not how You'd like it to be mate.'
Doesn't mean that further down it won't be happy in Arambubble!
We're not attached to it so there's No reflection ~ Psyche seeds.
A good friend but not a Lover ~ Stop your conditioning racing ~
She's having a Rebirth ~ burning everything with all the chains!
Phoenix rising from the flames, her streaming dynamic energies.
She's resonating telekinesis with the place ~ Glowing, growing.
The flame kindled, don't get caught into thinking anything else!
Here to experience the joy, the joy of being Open, loving you ~
Under the Honey pot ~ tripped over, picked it up, Now Look!
"Get over yourself man!" ~ bringing it down to Earth

Just have to be what I already am

His Guru said 'You are Love, the Life, the Truth' & he believed him!
Just explaining it to yourself essentially more & more Inside insight.
Quantum Hipsters on the Triple C diet, cigarettes, coke and coffee!
We cannot wake up alone of course it's intrinsically a mystery!
High Definition, Path of Discovery ~ with every new step we take.
In the Sacred valley of Piss ~ the bridge was soaking underwater.
Feeling they Hi-jacked common sense how does something evolve?
"My role in life is to awaken their divine female principle energy in as
many as need to be woken" He said. "I know you Microdot Central"
"I've never taken it like that" ~ "And I haven't taken enough Acid!"
"We are the Revolution here" .... He carried his own DMT Bible.
She knows people who know how to travel on that Cosmic trip.
Addicted to the BUZZ not a Quest, just happens in its own Space.
Stamps and Lines only for the gormless, boggled the 5% brain!
"Who knows the Saraswati mantra in case of a dire Emergency?"
Just being with the harmonious ~ with No/Mind (Non/attachment).
This aspect of Shakti ~ Illuminating all other aspects of Shakti!
Entry point into the Experience ~This is God Now ~ No Separation.
This is What they don't want you to Know ~ It's hidden by Religions.
They can read your eyes, sense neural pathways in your heart beats;
those auras not in the Mind. Their Bandit Chemist ~ He's in the Band!
Age of Aquarius ~ worrying, Mother Earth's having a Heart attack!
Solar flares, layers of Love ~ plasma around in each of our cells.
Subliminally It's this Fear of Separation ~ from the Divine Bliss,
for everything **IS** already **NOW** ~ what Jesus felt in this Space!
Just the nature of duality ~ however you dream it & beyond.
He's describing ~ 'that * that' ~ Decalcifying Pineal glands.
Devotees of Shakti being the enlightened Cosmic creation.
Oneness again through funky Orgasms.
"Everything is absolutely taken care of ~
All this Love that I know that I am"
'This Love Is Unconditional'

I Love Love ~ Obviously a lot of people Love War!
Impossible to know the reasons behind the reasons behind reasons.
Roll with the blows get your own philosophies yu know what I mean?
Split up in a sandstorm and it was freezing, with the wrong crystals!
'If you've never had it you don't miss it' ~ Just dancing to the music.
"I couldn't stand it but I had to give him the respect of listening" Why?
"Are you happy to have Electricity in your Life?" Higher frequencies ~
Wanting to get more of the light, we're all in a bubble; bubbles burst!
Why doesn't the Dalai Lama tell us about the Shambala Spaceships ~
*Flying thru the Bardo, over etheric Tibet * If it's true isn't that Freedom?*
*

He gave them a bag of weed
Half baked Baba having a Tantric Tantrum.
"I've already seen the photos of Angkor Wat!"
"I just remembered the memory I already had"
Dreamt the dream before and lived it out ~
"It's the Stoner's age painting graffiti on walls"
"If they own you they can bill you" Regulations...
"I only paid for a TV license while I was married!"
"I never paid 'Window taxes' after I got divorced"
Having a Premonition being stuck again in Goa!
It's good for you to love things.
A dreamer in the long grass.
*

A Lemon Ballerina on Benzodiazepin
Being spiked with the Fear ~ of dying.
"The python in the garden ate the kittens!"
'Birthday Card' ~ 'It's a Prison!" Doing time…
A Guide to our Galaxy ~ That will blow your Mind!
"Don't rub me the wrong way I've a genie in a jar of cherry jelly"
Subconscious association ~ Summer Love in a buttercup field.
Too good to miss! ~ Magically this got dragged into the story'
"I'm only the Angel ~"

Wall's Light-Minded Graffiti
Do You Wanna Live in Tantric Town with me?
All possible as soon as you come onto that frequency ~
From Boynton Canyon's Vortex ~ going over the heart.
Falling into the Unconditional Love ~ Oneness' vibration.
You have to allow the decision to fall into ~ the Intention.
Discernment, "I want It" And she's not Mad she's Mental!
This Silent Revolution coming from Inside out!
As soon as you're in it there's No going back ~
*Her father is a surreal Poet * birds on the beach*
*

'Psysick Ward'
"I'm too fucked up, give me the poison that I love"
"In front of you is a Torture machine…..!"
"Do you know what a vicious circle is?"
"Numptees, firing 50 Katoucha Rockets at you willy nilly!!!"
'Puts his soul in his pregnant girlfriend as he's dying moving thru Tokyo!'
*Being, doing impossibilities * "I do" ~ the whole thing is like an Acid trip.*
Beside Ma Ganga, Varanasi, surrendering! "I do" drinking Shiva's magic!
Wearing feathers, "I can't wear leather if I don't eat meat"
"He paid his death duties in advance avoiding any stress!"
Fanaticism gets you nowhere ~ 'This Is for Everyone'
*

COSMIC * LOVE ~ Is Cosmic Conception
Computerised reflections of your Mind ~ the Space for Time.
Only the moment is in the moment ~ living essentially Truth.
You can't step in the changing river twice at the same instant.
Everything is new cannot be repeated ~ being here right now.
Take the whole prana in & breathe Love out ~ Thankfulness.
Transformational ~ happy for Yourself and for all the others.
In gracious gratitude of the beingness more than the doing.
It's in-between what happens finding the divine in their hearts

"Taking My Trance Very Seriously"
"I never had a bad party at the Lotus"
Going to the next level of Telepathy…
"Is there a crystal on your forehead?"
Eternally is Space ~ it's real.
"I'm off the Chais!"

*

Primitive Cum * Sweet Stars
Witness it ~ living it ~ being it. Gazing at Luna's hot landscapes.
Right Context; It's allowing through creative Language ~ poetry.
People getting them to transcend ~ giving them the experience
of shattering illusions, their fantasies and delusions and fears.
Going over edges, through any limits, breaking Idols & taboos.
Showing them divine, feminine blissful climaxing, makes it real
you touch the same sublime, hard core, erotic, sexual ecstasy.
Full on Primal light will take you through your Cosmic Avatars.
Altruistic, multi dimensional ~ multi Orgasms will pull you up…
Feeling delicious inspiration ~ passionately fucking in the sand

*

Anti - Gravity Serendipity!
"I'm not gonna get any trouble from Babylon am I?"
The doctor told him that ~ "passion was endangering his life!"
Conceptual Tomatoes cloned to death, with no natural essences.
An amazing sky, last thing to see before going ~ into angel's dust.
It's everything to do with empty Space ~ with an Opening Channel!
No Thinking ~ I'm dreaming the dream, playing the main character
In the middle of a monstrous hill of banana bullshit; Full on Chaos!
Could be worse! Worse than dead? Let's have Peaceful Wisdom.
Just go with feeling ~ Minding Conscious SPACE, enjoys smiling.
'The Light of Love Coming Shining Through' ~ All Together in you.
The Space between the words is the feeling ~ don't need any words.
Feeling the feeling ~ speaking for Itself ~ as Abstract Expressionism

Vitality * Reality

'Neti Neti' not this or this in the Consciousness Space ~ of who I Am
Don't think ~ STOP! "I don't Know ~ let it be, the unknown energy"
Stop all the distractions of the Mind ~ Thinking, thinking, judging.
Take away the Thinking and we're left with only Conscious Space
which is always there translucently, in listening, in looking ~ being.
All I got was Orbs * be it don't know it in all the Mass Conditioning!

*

Soul Connected to Source

She was projecting on me ~ split, lost her Trust & Respect.
Asked her for Clearance, drinking in the process of her Art.
I read, felt a lot of her favourite vibrational channelings ~
Tuning into the frequency of the higher planes.
Where are you in the whole being ~ MAO Inhibitor?
Changing the World with four strand DNA children.
Waking us up over the dawning light ~ I love his voice.
All the Galaxies are now going through that reflection too.
Baking it from the Inside out ~ there is no more going back.
Mother nature is now getting it on with Solar Consciousness.
Opening up the diamond Brain * synchronising my hemispheres.
Spacey Molecules swimming across the timeless Milky Way.
Centring through the whole night
Rebalancing her crystalline head

*

Her Mystical dark side

Poisonous Scorpions on the sea cliff terrace living in a coke bottle.
The World is full of beautiful experiences ~ Allowance now to let go.
Ego dissolving whether you want to give it any consciousness or not.
The Flower of Life becomes through your body ~ your healing matrix.
Freely to Express ~ free to do what you want to do in peacefulness.
Nature's shrine to Hippies living on the beach in perfect harmony.
All my Chakras singing to every cell in her glowing, soft pink Lotus

Turmeric Moon

They all want a fair bride ~ An Intact Hymen, a healthy womb!
"We'll take your daughter to the doctor and see she's healthy"
Trying to figure out your innocent wife who was given to you
with a dowry; to love and cherish forever in honour and Trust.
She carried the smell of Jasmine and you battered her to death!
Who do you think she really is in relationship to you in this Universe?
Coming with a lifetime guarantee from Shakti.
How to tell you without it sounding too blasé!
If you're stupid enough to break your heart ~
She seemed like a devoted pragmatist to me!

*

*'Spread Em * Expose Em'*

Keeps making it up, Freedom to have no thought, force fed by a Matrix!
How can you quantify your life's journey ~ in experience, in allowance?
All the insider Satanists invested in unnatural irradiated Biotech stocks.
Praises the laurels of Genetically modified papadams not Panjandrums
as Safe to eat; "I gave it to my wife and children!"
"Nothing to regenerate so she slipped away!"
"All we can do is transcend the swamp"
by being in the stillness ~ in its Silence.
Feeling it really doesn't matter, spiritually.
You'll get out ~ If you struggle you'll sink!
"She's the least restrained Indian I ever met"
Describing natural Instincts in empty places.
Knowing the tree's deva energy of a sacred wood.
It reveals Spirit ~ wild horses talking to the Babylonian's.
Protesting the destruction of their lovely environment...
by unsympathetic humans in giant metal caterpillars!
Chopping down the last ancient Oak. WHY?
Almost like Magic those horses knew ~
Makes you cry!

Sadhguru Truth In Confusiopolis

No Religion ~ No Dogma, no separation, dividing-conquering!
Find it the way it works for you. The future is a joke.
"Here's my story" ~ See what the Universe provides.
Hybrids of Pachamama mixed with Union Vegetalis.
Place on the edge of the Jungle with all the Ayuhuasca
you can drink! A full re-emerging into Shakti's Divinity.
Fear of letting go ~ is the fear of letting go ~ of this life,
Mind, body thing; Off the grid * that was some amazing Illusion!
Permaculturist DMT. aficionados ~ fluttering with Mariposas in bliss.
The more people putting out Positive Propaganda the better. "YES!"
Don't give up just because they seem to Control most of the Media.
Dissolving together ~ burning together on the sacred fire!
Maintaining the energy in the Space ~ Psychedelic valley.
The oil is black, the soil is alive, look at it ~ it's nature.
And we're it and it's Perfect

*

DMT Verity

I have to see God as being in everyone else.
You only get it when it's Not Understandable ~
It's Not the Word there's Nothing to remember or know.
FEELING IT ~ What you FELT no words for it * SPACE.
Absolute without any of the Identificationing; Just want to
be empty and see what it is without my Ego Formulating it.
They THINK what their Mind is tellin' them ~ what to do?
Bringing awareness to really appreciating health, Love ~
Everything leaves you one way or another ~ even my wife.
Realising it's all temporary, there's no*thing there ~ but life!
"If you don't leave it ~ it leaves you!"
Energy becoming Aware of Itself ~
Consciousness being Infinite Space.
Life is our teacher ~ Dying is natural
Silently tuning within Spiritual essence

Metaphorically
'War On Terrorism'
'War For Terrorism'
'War Is Terrorism!'
"Forget about Terrorism we're now melting, being in the Love"
"It's who is doing the medicine!" ~ Hearts & Eagles in the fire!
*

Opium Cough Mixture
"I had two Math's teachers that I made cry"
"Amazing, depends on which drugs you're on!"
"Really happy, he's pulling in the energy for us to drive on"
Sublime music, really nice rituals ~ blooming up, centering.
Transmuting Creativity ~ dancing with the Phoenix's feathers
*

A Night of Paranoia
Gratuitous Violence begets Collateral Murder!
"I'm not a revolutionary I'm a way of life"
"Are you a lump of meat?"
We are Transcendental!
*

Pure * Code
Going into making Fridge Magnets.
Taking responsibility for your self
"It can't exist without dualism ~
in the Mind bringing Love & painful
Identifying ourselves with mass suffering"
Don't have to be thinking ~ takes it all away from **Space**.
Quarantine this Mad Mind, made of Self, ME ~ creates us!
Illness has to have a cure as it's from a natural polar state.
Sages femmes, treating them as Pagan Goddesses ~ surely
not getting rid of the women just to destroy their knowledge?
This Consciousness process brings on the Peace!

Cowboy Bullet Proof

Coke bottles causing anger ~ a glass meteor landed in the Kalahari!
"They're shooting at us heart attacks ~ with Frequency weaponary"
The biggest reptiles coming out of the deepest shit holes.
"You can only know 'Insanity' from being Sane yourself!
People looking at you when you get this big thing out... e a s y ~
one eyed snake. Rather be natural, trippy hippy than a Neo Nazi.
Ganpatti, as soon as there's an Obstacle ~ Whooooooosh!
He loves rice pudding and sweet almond, mango dumplings.
"None of it is Real!" If it was Real it wouldn't change but it does ~
The Guantanamo shuffle at Club X RAY how f....Real is that still?
Genocide is crazy; to get ONE man, Sadman Hussein, started a WAR!
How you ever gonna have Peace with No Trust in their genes for eons?
Mind-Sets ~ new Hi-Viz Experimental Material! Another infidel lynching..

*

"Baba this way!"

"You're a truly unique connection on the river"
Relationships are about relating' self existing Truth, in Tantric Ville.
"Did I win you or buy you as a slave?" "I bought my wife's freedom!"
Something beautiful and lovely ~ Its turned into a nightmare for me!
At the bottom holding everyone else up ~ She is the germinating seed.
"When the lust starts to fade" Depends how much you Love each other.
Free adaptation of a Classic; "I Love this track"
"I wanna give some good ~ good Lovin."
The trip's started ~ NOW!
"Feel Me" ~ she said

*

That Man from Peru

Shivaratri then it's Parvati's Psytrance night!
Appearing from an unidentifiable Celestial Orb.
"Just found some space then You f... well turned up on the Planet!"
Peace and Quiet, forever, maybe; singing Divine nature all the time ~
18 years old with no feelings ~ "MeMeMeMe" no time to take a breath!

Fucking Up People's Codes

TV. Chill out, Brainwashing, Conditioning, Scrambling your Mind!
Sucks your energy, makes you a couch potato, tells you to believe
what they say, made it interactive ~ "Tell us all 'bout your Inner self"
You'll have to be very underground! Dystopian, FEAR PROGRAMS.
The Judge will be a big Mother-Board; What do they want from us?
'Awareness is equanimously feeling the Space that the FORMS are in'
Decide which Identity to feed y/our mind, to react with such a behavior!
'The Indian President educated himself on a railway platform.'
Different motivation, intent is reality ~ a missile is not a rocket!
Teaching 'Computer Hacking'..... 10000R in Bombay, to kids.
Space*ships have to TRANSCEND ~ we're going to other Planes.
This or that hallucinogenic galaxy, another Cosmic, comic book…
That's one view of the future but the future doesn't exist ~
We all got a free choice but soon there won't be with ID. #s.
Government controls choice 'To be chipped or not to be chipped?'
Then they'll know everything about You ~ Scanning everyone's ~
See you in virtual reality, Your whole Life meta Data, Profile potential.
Now tell us this! They'll even know if you are telling the Truth or not!
A blip on a screen*Exact Locationing, never getting lost in the jungle!
IT'S INSIDE YOU ~ ALL THE BEST * KEEP IT REAL

*

It's < LIGHT > Waves
The Sun Illuminates ~
Just being in Infinite Space
* It's All Inside You *
Here (0) now Universe

*

Bliss frequency
We know what we want.
Light shows you Truth
Loving the Moment ~

<u>Of the Unknown</u>
500 TIMES X THE OBSESSIONAL!
IN The Box is the MIND & KARMA.
It's ALL rattling around Inside ~
Open it up feeling infinity of Zero Space
Space Inside ~ being ~ Space outside.
Let it flow in Oneness for the good of all.
"I've got a dying man lying on my floor!"
"Sorry I have to be selfish here ~ "
Wanting a little more time on Earth
even if it's Hell or Heaven ~
Not enough free Unconditional Love!
"Please forgive me but it's Time to go"
In Living the Art of Transcendence
*

<u>Blue Platinum Harbour</u>
It got mixed up and Controlled, what the Seers brought over ~
Man made Law is not what every man has ~ Common Sense.
Just fall in, this is Mother Earth, now fall in the fire ~ "I Love It!"
& Transmute ~ Wanting to lose Yourself in the Houses of Love…
*Less density * more Clarity ~ no holding on, leaving this dimension*
puts pieces of wood in the sacred flame, something else comes up.
You don't put the Conditions ~ not Conditional, no duality, no Mind.
You fall in the One space ~ burning in the violet, white, golden light.
Wants to be in the rainbow, wants to go off in a woman like a Rocket!
Has to be penetrated by millions of sperm ~ One of them makes it!
It's Consciousness, pure life energy feeling its Love ecstasy ~
Coming from Creation ~ making Unconditional Love is Greatest

Sacred * Nature

Oil is the blood of Mother Earth ~ more Earthquakes are coming!
No lubrication, jelly ~ easing the rubbing Tectonic plates' friction!
Harmonic Pachamama living on the 5th dimension and showing us
how to go with it or lose it ~ Pushing out your energy in any direction.
Lie down and see how much it unfolds then you see different positions.
Have to allow the Soul Frequency to take us over ~ our * I AM * Space.
Presence still connected to the Cosmic Spiritual Divine ~ Reintegrating
with what's coming up ~ have to look inside the more you will discover.
You have it all in yourself ~ existential Earth Sparking, unknown codes.
All time now is ~ changing, waking up, remembering what we've lived.
Out of the BOX ~ no more Brainwashing, we can go as far as we want.
As Omni*versal as we allow*Omnipresence*Omnificent*Omnipotence
I'm with you in the ONE

*

Emotion ~ in Motion

"Esoterically, empirically manifested ~ a tree from out of a little seed.
By free will, big bunch of bananas ~ You don't have to put it in a box.
It is Truth, it's not me talkin' it's comin' through me, over my feeling ~
Space ~ I know I'm telling the Truth it's not my Mind Control speaking"
Love's direct energy not the constant word, it's in-between the words.
And it makes only sense ~ that is in the emotional.
This is it you want to be on the lightest frequency ~
You are multi dimensional, 3rd 4th 5th onto infinity
All as One transmuting energy

*

Common Senses

'Thoughts are Ultimately expressed by Love' What is the feeling feeling?
1st Chakra, Practical, the Bankers; 2nd Government, laws; 3rd Religion;
Consciousness from the breaking light * Sun's rays ~ Love is the Fuel.
"Nothing more to do than to be" ~ Is feeling heart ~
Only to look at yourself, take time to go inside
because everything is changing in the vortex ~

Genetic * Kinetic * Tantric * Shamanic

Penetration Dive ~ Infinite Rainbows... trippy Love arising.
Kundalini is the life force you fill up all the Loving light cells.
It's the biggest Blessing but we make such a fuss ~ egoist,
we do nothing about it. Everyone is dancing the dance, but
"don't ask me, I'd rather tease you, get you hot then f... off!"
What sort of HAPPINESS do You want ~
WHO WANTS TO BE CONTROLLED?
Have to Live it Yourself now ~ no excuse.
Bit of an Overload ~ It all falls in as it is.
We have to make this Unconditional step
then take this Tantric Sacred approach ~
*

Its Originality!
That's energy ~ coming off the wall through shapes and colours.
It's just expressions of how you feel ~ Resonance convergence.
Thank God for Polarity trance dancers tuning us into Zero Space!
"In out, in out ~ shake it all about"
It's the acceptance of the Mystery
that's the answer ~ to the Mystery
*

Flick It On*You can't go back
Thought I needed a Structure ~ I did and it became....
Meanings ~ Expression, what's Inside is just swirling ~
"Make the unselfish eye an Emerald green and that will be beautiful"
Pachamama walked to the end of the World because she's worth it!
Sacred Geometric flames * Creation in this dynamic flower of Life.
No colour wheels, no demarcation lines of separation ~ just Space

HAPPY COSMIC TRAVELS
You can't know who 'YOU' are without duality making the Object ~
*Embrace nothing ~ Letting go of structure * Is the Universal Mystery.*
My Zero energy is not separate from this Space ~ It is this SPACE!
Looking with your Whole ~ being feeling.
There's nothing really there but Awareness ~
because it's the wholistic Space of Love's Awareness.
Going into the Unknown ~ is where you really 'KNOW'
Embrace not Knowing ~ this Amazing, beautiful MYSTERY.
*It's only words, we can't know what it is*We Are It ~ essence.*
How could you possibly KNOW what you are?
*
Networks > Enjoy Social Engineering <
Somehow you feel Bigger than what's happening ~ just happening.
I Accept the Pain ~ Consciously Aware of the Pain ~ rippling in out.*
Natraj there's a lot more going on in Our Universe ~ so you let it go.
Can you touch any boundaries, these feelings give a sense of Grace?
Tuning yourself into that Magic place ~ just Truth happening in Space
Taking you out of this thing happening ~ is a tool of transformation
*
Being Absent Minded
How rich or poor do you have to be to let go?
The Moon is the Target, the one who's aiming, pointing at it is You ~
Watching it, she can't take you to the Moon; You have to go Yourself!
*Seeing oneself observing * awareness, Your Intent is Creating Reality ~*
We're in many different places at the same time ~ ask a holist physicist.
*What do we ultimately connect to? We're all Multi * Dimensional entities.*
Omnipresent on Jupiter, Omnipotence on Mars, Omnificence in Venus.
Making the right connection; Contact ~ frequency, then You're in it!
Earth & Sky kissing each other ~ letting go all over.
3D. will be in the way ~ "I'm going for Flying Yoga"

Pieces of the Cake

Now putting the Magic into action and living it.
Looking into her soul ~ not a therapy session.
Unconditional Love ~ get out of your own way.
Just close your eyes ~ you know the black stuff.
"Can you take me with you on holiday Please!"
Be true to Yourself ~ not running behind the same GM. carrot!
'Since you are the way you are ~ because that's how you are.'
Every one lives how they want to live ~ You have to ask them.
*Getting in the line ~ Align yourself in Spirit * higher frequency.*
Giving yourself the rope ~ Smile, remember You Are FREE.
'If you kill animals you don't get into the Unconditional Love'
This is friendship ~ giving him discernment, making him aware,
on The Borderline ~ "Fuck I've pissed him off"
We have to change this Idea, 'It's You & Me'
We Are One ~ we can't separate it anymore.
We're cutting something out for ourselves.
It's all One ~ It's ZERO SPACE

*

Pan's Comet

*Up & down the Higher Sub*Conscious Principle.*
'The deeper you go the higher you fly'
Opening the Gates to Mother Earth ~
Luminescent glowing sky blowing their Minds.
Cobalt blue, white, platinum ray ~ frequency.
Different refractions of light ~ Perspectives.
Different qualities, Solar bonbons, energies.
Feeling Appreciation not the last Invasion ~
of My Space ~ YOU Know you're a guest!
Women wailing in the Heart of the Eclipse.
OK I see that it's broken ~ ORGASMLESS!

Too Drunk to Pay

'Don't Fuck with the rare Elephants!'
They're gentle unless they get drunk ~
Attacked by an Emu, In an Indian Zoo.
"I don't eat anything from the sea ~"
You touch it and something happens.
Fukushima Aliens being evacuated!

*

Roman Reich

Satanists, lost all sense of human naturalness ~
All the perversions but you don't pay Monseigneur!
And here is someone who's truly listening ~
The respect of not Invading her Space.
Letting go of a belief is harder, they say!
The Catholic church in Control of Psychological Warfare!
What sort of agreement was made with the other sides?
I go with you this way on the journey of life ~
Living in the moment ~ Enjoy it while you can!
"I had to powder his girlfriend" ~ A good touch.
"What would you do if you were in my shoes?"
Came to his point, realizing his feelings...

*

Bless the Spirit

The moment put in music ~ Pure Crystals.
Best of all for everyone ~ over the Sunlight.
Transmuting Solar DNA. ~ to do it for yourself.
Through that you give out the Love to everyone.
In Realness ~ Opening up your complete heart.
We are cooking in the Sunrays, becoming ~
more and more refined,
Cosmic Jeweled beauty

Beach Bom Shankar
"Why do we do what we do?"
"We're awake with the light"
Energy coming from the early morning rays ~
'He turned out as Einstein and couldn't get a Job!'
"We have been proper, Fully BRAINWASHED ~
Can't comprehend, imagine anything different!
*Powers keeping us out of being * AWARENESS.*
Lost in Selfish Ego we lose sight of the Space Life.
Goes out of the Wonder to conflictions of the Mind!
This feeling is JOY when you're Not Thinking of It!
'Finding the Miracle when You Are the Miracle!'
Being part of everything Alive
*

Their Bread & Butter
Notice the Silence ~ Stillness is eternal SPACE.
AWARENESS Is the ESSENCE ~ Just letting it be.
Non Conceptual, Pure Consciousness ~ Sensations of Grace.
*Always seeing Objects not Zero*SPACE that the Objects are in!*
Remembering You Are Alive ~ there is nothing else.
Awareness of this full Energy field not the delusions.
Not obsessed by the barking dog ~ it's just a sound.
Let it ALL go ~ we're left with primordial emptiness
*

'I AM Orgasm' ~ Not Egoism
Sublime rhyme, Harmony is harmony ~ Divine is divinity!
Slipped on a wet patch ~ nice to pass out on the beach.
Light ~ you are an Angel flying in Love's Sweet Spot.
*Invoking the purple flame * Send in the Next Level!*
Danced on raw chocolate, full power ~ wavy edges.
Being fully Radiant ~ receiving Vibrational Ecstasy

"I went straight from Hilltop to the Airport!"
It's all about the energy ~ dancing.
"I want my 24 hours ~ In Goa!
Trance Party ~ Full Power"
*

Self Awareness ~ Open Space
The Stasi revamped, 'Reality TV' series spying into all of your orifices.
Listening to the Tapes of ordinary people to find any secret cracks!
Singing the Kali not the Saraswati mantra when in mortal danger!
Getting clearer, she can't hold any longer her Reptilian face!
Seeing ~ over feeling comes the knowing of the Matter.
"We shine the light of consciousness just by Smiling"
Feeling her exciting Impulses ready to explode!
Waking up to Motorhead ~ we had our phases!
"I wanna Psychedelic Om"
*

Bloody Red Cooperpedy
'White man digging a (BIG FUCKIN') HOLE!'
Getting your Dynamite License, blasting the stones!
Opal fires shining in every colour of Peyote rainbows…
Tuning in to the Higher frequencies ~ everyone was melting.
Have to hold it up in you; An honour to be at his Eco fireplace.
Giving Full Power to the flames of transmutation ~ needs the milieu.
Old soul you got it all in your genes ~ you got more Pleiadian angles.
Gave you energy ~ made me weep like a bitch!
Underlying emotions ~ different* different* same.
It's All Vibrational healing ~ we're getting baked from the Inside out.
Over the feeling, Truth shows the other ones in their infinite Fractal.
The Silent Revolution... of becoming more light ~ being enlightened,
seeing in light, being this Moon not a finger pointing to the Moon!

Full Re*emerging Into* Shakti
Her lovely wildflowers withered and died....
Reflections of ~ **'The Human Condition'**
Horrendous or Wondrous ~ Being ~ neither ~
Continuously changing ~ unchanging, changing.
Refocusing my intention on what I want, good
for me ~ not me fighting against the system!
It is as it is ~ at this moment of infinite Space.
Be detached from making any value judgments,
It doesn't make more sense ~ **Be That FEELING.**
It's more than a fine conception of spirituality
*

Cosmicgasms In Cosmicville
Met a Chillum making tantric massage Baba for a Masala chai.
Ultimately it is to be transcended into the Divine
Once they can recognize that it's just energy.
Enlightening these other states of Orgasm ~
Rising up from the root chakra to the heart
from the ethereal to Love and Compassion
up to the Pineal gland releasing its DMT.
Then you're back to the Absolute ~
reconnects you with ~ who You are
*

Gnostic Now
From before Shiva ~ before Shakti.
All Supra*realities have gone into ONE
Just Is and being one of many versions.
Just choose which bit you wanna believe.
"Do not believe a word I gotta say ~
Drop the history of thought ~ Allowing
EXPERIENCE ~ to be

Ugly, Fat & Old UFO's

Heard two Ketamine Twins, foaming at the mouth, doing blueys!
"Everyone else was trippin and I was MDMA*mazed!"
"If I can't dance to it then I'm not going to play it!"
What's goin' on in the back of their heads is a mystery!
Just caught the biggest Jellyfish off the coast of Japan
Radioactivity made them all flipping, clicking Hot Tuna.
Killed all Aquatic life ~ get your head around that!
She was the Chief Slaughter man's daughter.
'The brightest light makes deepest shadows'
And had to be revived

*

"We Can Still Be Friends"

What does it mean to have Individual consciousness ~
Bringing Christ down to Earth ~ thru the Inspirational Gate.
With a Sense of Mind ~ Self, creating a beautiful Mosaic.
Capturing the Social energy ~ the Mystical vernacular.
Found himself in front of a Crucifiction, all very surreal!
Who wants to inherit this Toxic dump * of Planet Earth?
He once was a Master of Mass persuasion ~ confusion;
Worships a Fuhrer who was a Megalomaniac and You?
It's all an Illusion being played on the stage of your Mind
which is being witnessed by your infinite consciousness ~
Frescoes representing the power of Images as y/our Reality!
Confronting delusions with more contradictions ~ for an answer!
Why are you denying your body senses, flagellation of Thought
to comply with suffering not the ecstasies of vital, flesh dualities?
They have No feeling ~ human empathy, oblivious to the radiance.
Hell on Earth ~ unless you're transcended in the here * now.
"Healthy Mind ~ Healthy Body" shining in the Spiritual eye.
Being All In the multi * dimensional Oneness

Ambassador Frequency

'Everything has been captured and enraptured in Sunlight'
'Stopped the Carnival for making too much noise in Anjuna!'
'The Inquisition Never Sleeps' ~ Climbing the Wall of Energy,
Vibration ~ "They don't hunt and kill for Pleasure like we do."
It's all about FEELINGS ~ in your Morphic * Resonance Field
"Cosmic will always throw it for you because your hand is Open"
"Being able to overcome all the Obstacles in my Life!"
"We can become HAPPY within Ourselves"
Transforming Yourself ~ Eternal Bliss.
'NAM NYOHO RENGE KYO'

*

Not Poor ~ PURE!

Too High * 3000 signals happening to you in any moment!
Price of Globalisation ~ Chemtrails poisoning a clear sky!
Individualised Programming for the Greedy Self -Therapy.
Having a Panic Attack in the Mind!
"I don't Trust Doctors anymore!"
"I got BOOBS too ~ Look at me!"
Replacing metal for Ceramic fillings.
Biodegradable, smart non fluoride teeth!

*

She's Astronomical!

Something you Never forget ~
Learning to walk ~ learning to talk.
Survival Instinct swimming ~ with the fishes,
having a natural child*birth in an azure lagoon.
Human Evolution along ~ Love's stepping stones.
Learning from our mistakes ~ Riding his hologram bicycle to Sirius.
Being the moment ~ asking the Dakini Oracle a rhetorical question;
64 female Goddesses dancing around me ~ this Zero point * Is it True?

Armageddon's Trauma
'Friendly fire' the Canadians lost 600 at Caen ~ made it into a ruin!
War Hero's nerves ~ constant fighting no respite! Who set this up?
I'll never forget it, 15,000 killed or wounded in his first fire fight!
You can get Killed any second ~ their children can be mutilated!
Resolved ~ Unquestioning obedience to authority and hierarchy!
Worshipping the foremost Patron saint of soldiers at the Cenotaph!
This is Classified; For your eyes only. Telling each other Top secrets!

*

Zephyr * Zodiac
Sunbeam Rapier, Singer Gazelle, Hillman Minx, Corsair, Consul, Capri.
A salmon pink Daf coupe, pale blue Reliance Scimitar, green Riley.
Nothing but the Government's Economic decisions, disasters!
"It's about prices on the World Market that's all."
You own her ~ time, paying her superannuation.
'We got a mountain gorilla in our back garden'

*

You Just Know It In the Heart and Are Connected
Fluoride Pills for Pregnant women at Your local Eugenics Farmacy!
National Anthems ~ Brainwash Us More! "Who is Ruling this Earth?"
Went to the Department of Official Propaganda; Orwellian Section 4.
Looking for a Mental landscape to bang my head against; Or Not!
"The more you know the more painful it is!" Really? Until it lets go ~
"Take my sister home with you she's got nowhere to stay tonight!"
They're passing out on MDMA. ~ I'm high as a kite on Cannabis oil!
"Let me die for my Emperor!" Who's that nutter High on "Banzai"?
But the Spirit's always there ~ Your MIND becomes the Channel
for you to become a butterfly ~ to be a bird and fly with the birds.
A feeling of Peace flowing through it, nice makes you feel Aware.
Looking just there as a Human being ~ You're born Free
and then they CONDITION-Control, Master-You,
Breaking your Spirit ~ taming a wild horse!

The Blue Yoni

You jump on a Crystal and tune it in to where you want to go ~
And there You are in Space. An Oversoul secret*peregrination.
The 'I AM' Presence, structure in your birth, Akashi recordings.
It's coming out of You… bring it in the 'I AM NOW PRESENCE'
It has Form ~ the Gift of God and myself as a Gift of God to give.
Transformation body relaxing, Theta healing, seeing a white light.
You Consciously are falling in Space and give Yourself Space.
You dissolve your little Form ~ it's lying there dreaming the dream
but you're not there ~ Witnessing Spirit, You're more than the body!
You are your own Satguru God ~ Free flow not Controls of your Ego.
You're listening to What? Me & Everything ~ Everything is Me.
I'm freely Integrated In Love & Love Is Space

*

'Prefers Cock to Peptic'

"Sex is like havin' a shit ~ A natural Bodily function..."
"Whoa hold on a sec. but they do have some romance!"
'Every village has a Karaoke Bar ~ turned it into a 'Happy House'
"Then the Americans came along after Bombing it, turned it into R&R."

*

The Gandhi Massive!

Coming to the 'WE' the 'wei*wei' Awareness.
Now it comes from Itself ~ we see we knew nothing of Spirit…
Emotional healing ~ You are the Creator of It, enjoying the light.
You can only heal yourself, they can show the way ~ let go.
You don't have to believe it, just have to experience it ~
Everyone has the right to live out what they want, just be.
Did the healer take away your Pain - And all the Suffering?
Can't go backwards, it's a hierarchy, he might be Hanuman!
There is no better or worse ~ only frequency, Divine Consciousness.
Bringing lower up to make you higher ~ all about energy in the chain

Cosmic Psyche*delicate Tribe
"In the balance is the inner peace"
His shoes were diamonds ~ A full crystal room to break the Idea
that holy men can't have the material ~ 'Opposition to Love is Fear'
He could hold it up because he put himself out of the emotional game.
Illusion's crackin', Alien frequencies coming out; spread the message.
Even if it's just a glimpse, people feel this picture's vibrational energy.
More than the seeing, it's immediate reflection more than the attention.
'It goes infinitely out ~ infinitely in, somewhere they meet' in spirals.
*You have to call the Magic in * You are the Magician now!*
Intent is becoming reality
*

This is the Green Ship!
You lose yourself in the emotion ~ perfecting quartz.
Try and stay in the centre of spinning Mother Earth.
Drop a stone in a pond ~ the ripples reach everywhere;
In us, with us, through us we carry it around as us ~
'Happiness is in the allowance of the happening'
It is what it is ~ being very happy
*

Was Quite Hard
Surfing through Star gates ~ of Compassion & Mercy with yourself.
Creating a New Language, a new code, new sub ~ consciousness.
Taking our bio-brains out of the diabolical and setting them free ~
Wanting to convey the feelings ~ our senses of natural harmony.
Physical and metaphysical ~ dualities in tune with the full moon.
'Are you seeing the inner light shining from your Mind's eye?'
Are you feeling Abstract Awareness ~ or are you a lost soul atom?
Seven planets in Scorpio, she is deep; I had to learn to let her go ~
"You have the whole life with her, then I knew nothing could be lost,
had to let her go again on that soul frequency ~

Toy girls with benefits
"I wouldn't work anywhere where they didn't give me coffee!"
You can just smell the decaying dreams ~ Anti climbing monkey paint.
No one's working and full of Scag at the pantomime and illuminations!
Skanky dead fuck- Whores! The Pleasure Beach ~ all gone wrong.
No Surrendering ~ dancing to Psy trance at the Tower!
*

'Injuries consistent with a Tiger attack!'
The Vatican, Biggest arms sellers; who'd like constructive criticism?
"The Carnival Is Over" ~Take off the red shoes and red horns Baba!
Kissing the feet of an Imprisoned Moslem woman; Why do it now?
Flicking a forked Tail. "You never know how the Malai Kofta will be!"
*

Blasphemy from the Dark Ages
Pagans enraptured by the scent of Jupiter's arse; Brand DNA.
Ayatollah State of Iran ordered Muslims to kill Salman Rushdie.
'Employ everything you got to send him to Hell' Self-destructive
frame of Mind, terrorism from the mosque to freedom of thought.
'Satanic Verses' ~ publicly burned in Bradford! A city in England!
"Violence begets Violence mate." Having a Fatwa in Lancashire.
Vilification, Freedom of speech not allowed in this country again.
A Heretic, 'When in Wigan do as our Ahmed not as the Wigans'
or you'll be condemned to death, filleted his throat by a chippie!
Their honor ruined his life, murdered for the insult & the shame.
Buddhists can talk about anything even God ~ Human solidarity.
Fundamentalism gone mad, strict rules, burnt as a meat pie Love.
More Inquisitors in the name of Religion still torturing the 'infidels'.
Separation & duality couldn't make it to forgiveness & compassion.
The Sun & all celestial bodies revolving around the Earth or else!
They discovered the orbits of the stars but burnt their telescopes
tonight & are rampaging on the streets with other demagogues!
*

R. Mahashi ~ 'Never mind the mind' ~ 'You're always in the heart'

We Are the Space ~ Ship inside

*Merkaba in Alignment to go * going up there, Celestial Spirals*
Close your eyes, you're spinning in vibrating Space ~ Inside.
Inside as Outside ~ as above so below polarities' vortexes.
*Observing the Stars * we are Stars * created through us.*
Auras of Cosmic energy fields ~ In Zero SPACE
All Loving frequency
*

Mr. Mystical

I couldn't help myself; She said, "Come over for a chillum"
Rebirth of the Planet ~ Ascending, all going up together.
In your Soul frequency ~ might have a bit of wobble
Transmuting, trance ~ juicing the Standing Wave.
Your personality is in danger of being gobbled up
if you don't think You have it ~ Hit by indefinable Sun flares!
Consciousness out of duality ~ inspiring the seed to flower.
Feeding us with all kinds of gifts to make us happy.
*"We don't seem to play Psy*trance in the house."*
Silent snowflakes falling inside colour fields.
On those wavy telepathic wavelengths ~
*

Free to Rome

Contaminated Paella Bonds. Topsy Turvy Defaulting, web links.
Demanded their money from an emptied vault; Thick as thieves!
Predatory lenders IOU's as good as Gold! Who do you believe?
'Thrive, Corporation, Zeitgeist Adbusters, alternative networking.'
Greed, weakness at the heart of an insane Profligate Euro Zone.
People who come from very Impoverished backgrounds wear?
Insane Hyper-debt, Corrupt Banksters, Political criminals' lobby.
Another systemic Corporate Raid, Ignorant, autocratic Predators.
Check out 'Inside Job' They'll make you fight for every fuckin' cm!
Elites, Cryptocrats, Plutocrats wanting control of World's New Order

Heart Drive

"I gave up ~ I want to see my soul mate"
Out 'til 2am with the frauleins from Stuttgart.
If you're in the jail, you go Astral, it's so simple.
Tuned in to Higher frequencies ~ listen to the silence
hear the Universe sing ~ 'TUTTI FRUTTI'
"Don't wanna run around like a Cock!"
"You have to give to the Higher Self"
"I wanna be a Tantric Templar"

*

Unconditional Love

The 2nd coming of Christ ~ the Crystal grid, through us.
Duality doesn't make sense anymore; Program failure!
200 Tanks hanging out in each Metropole; They go with the Riot!
You see Hell from the remotest places every night on the TV. News!
'Some of our new viewers may find the Slaughter Images distressing'
All opposite to what they say, can't believe this nonsense anymore!
"I respect how you are and you do what you gotta do." Just be kind!
It's Major, to let go ~ of the good and bad feelings, the expectations.
Psychic realms, Knowing how it is ~ It's the Zero energy ~ neutrons.
No longer Protons * electrons, falling now
In Zero and you fall in Unconditional Love

*

Distributing It Where?

Being in a Support group for the 'Over Qualified' ~Too cute!
'One ounce of Gold creates 30 tons of Toxic waste; Bumper dumper!'
Be free & go through ~ A CONSCIOUS PRIMAL SPACE experience
Have to get some appreciation ~ connecting to holistic awareness.
Blew my mind already, holding Realisation, knowin' your Allowance.
The 'Real Truth' has to come out! ~ 'There's Plenty for Everybody'
'She'll know exactly to let them know' ~ Gifts are coming

'The Unknown ~ Never knowing what's comin' at you next!'
Making us Fearful of what's out there ~ deep blue, the dark.
With horrors, monsters, scary aliens, terrorists from Mars.
"Pass the post apocalyptic Druid's magic holly wand mate"
"Of the future ~ I want a blonde with big tits living one free love,
experiencing the most beautiful tropical beaches on Planet Gaia.
XX Sci*fi, Propaganda, 'That was no fake 'Home Invasion' mate!'
They made it as a test, MK. Ultra, Matrix programs taking us over.
Who's the first freak to try Reindeer piss? Seeing the seams split.
Bowing down ~ alignment shifting to the centre of a spiral Galaxy

*

Nazi Mentality Dawn

Living under gas lights; Power & Money got all the Technology!
When the revolution comes these people are going to disappear!
Twenty million have died in Africa just the other day ~ Ritualistic stuff.
Forces of a king holding a lamb and him with a cloned cloven hoof!
'Men's best contraceptive ~ getting drunk and passing out!'
Satanic Imagery from the invisible satellites overhead.
"The only way to know the Unknown
Is to consciously, fully embrace it"

*

"I don't wanna go to Mapusa" & "I don't wanna go to Rocky St"

"They're just dripping in it, Gold, housewives from Karnataka!"
Investment in the bride, Your energy sticking to the karma side.
"Nothing beats a lovely African Asset…. I mean Sunset!"
There's a Mandrax dealer sat, guarding my back gate.
Everything is possible ~ when you're Free...
Free to be naked with me ~ in our Happy daze.
"Caning drugs, gettin' wasted, no problem at all"
"Lot of sticky stuff around last night"
'Feeling good everyone's a Winner'

Progressive Trance in Shanghai!
Different Vibe ~ different tribe, different reality!
"I'm the one who can smell her Wet seasons"
Wild Pheromones ~ blossoming in abundance
"It's the same bed but in two different Universes"
Now look for feeling ~ energy, not the appearance.
All we have to do is be one with no minds flowing.
No things blocking ~ distracting Consciousness
From the Central Sun ~ it's not Black Magic!
Looked in every Temple ~ the Love is within.
*

Prohibited on land ~ Bigotry's fine at sea
'Many methods of austerities, Yoga Asana, Torture…
We're having FUN for fuckin' sure! Full On - Off - On!
The Launch pad, straight out of body into the ethereal'
'Nothing is Solid it's all conceived in our Consciousness'
'Lock into it therefore so be it ~ embracing New SPACE'
Stay in the bliss whatever you hear, whatever happens,
being bombarded with shit to keep us in FEAR ~ Sanctioned.
'They've gone on their yachts to drink with playboy bunnies'
Call it Baksheesh, a gift, 'Bribes' 'Overseas Development Aid'
Getting 100 whip lashings on her Adulterated back in public ~
All bowing in the same direction then cutting each other's throat!
*

Ferocious Crusaders
A bunch of Murdering, sadistic, satanic bastards; Knights –
Templars all about War and Empire and killing all in their way!
Absolutely Ruthless, Top Illuminati managing God's holy relics.
Pick of the day, International Operations controlling the Planet.
All over the place ~ Management Systems! Satanic on the wall.
A broken Cross, Shock & Awe of War! Is it very Glorious to you?
It's appreciating your*self in the bliss ~ 'the Challenge of the day!'

"Me mate's taken my happy juicy hole off me...."
Like most cultures ... they are built on HIERARCHY.... even
tho' they proclaim Equal FREEDOM... policemen are smiling,
accepting their Commanding Officer's Rank, rights, his inherent
privilege, status. These Dualities, contradictions are what imprison
People's bodies & minds in the cages that they have allowed to be
created for themselves. They have accepted it even to the denial
of their Universal Spirit ~ so we are all locked in... to a MASSIVE
PSYCHOSIS, MASS CONDITIONING, IDENTITY.. CRISIS.
MANIPULATED by those who want to RETAIN this POWER
up to a POINT... Until something so abhorrent happens which
goes far beyond/against Human limits then we sheeples must
react! It's like being ordered to do something against our 'soul'
such as TORTURE, BEING TOLD TO SACRIFICE OUR OWN
LIVES OR OUR CHILDREN'S; We are TESTED each moment
TO COME TO SELF REALISATION & FREEDOM AND LIVE ~
Your life as you wish the World to be
*

Drop out ~ of Time

Realise the thoughts we were attached to, that they were Wrong.
Taking a walk at sunset through a field of wild flowers not Cyber
Space X FILES, Holographic Paranoid City; any Schizophrenia?
What's your REAL Name, where were you born, do you believe?
Are you Faithful, manipulated in a Power Game, the Art of War,
do you believe in Buddha, are you married to a Psy*chic lover?
Take the Escape hatch, eject as soon as you can AND DO NOT
LOOK BACK EVER * INTENTION TO LIVE IN * ABUNDANCE*
Same * Same, different to me ~ energy Levels of an inner view.
If you're gonna express anything * Karmic seeds are in bloom.
With roots & bark, concocting his superb psyche active brew,
expressing poetically ~ sublime beauty

Paranoia of Apocalypse ~ Bend Your Neck!
Leaving the body paralyzed ~ understanding what's goin' on!
Conscious whilst they drain your blood & hack your head off!'
Drugged with Amala seeds as precious sacrifices to their Idol.
"Praise be to our God the Almighty, the merciful." WHACK!
Appeases angry spirits! Stalking alien demons, habla espagnol?
Let's offer up some more human beings in a gruesome holy ritual!
'Killings gone wrong being done by an executioner in the mask'
In front of the Temple keep the offerings rolling down the steps.
Catastrophic, wrathful, Pachamama coming to teach us a lesson.
Hit by a Tsunami of retribution ~ being rescued from Obliteration!

*

Rampant Dragon
Overpowering them with a Honey trap, going beyond surfaces.
Dead simple; I give You the Authority to be in total control!
Emptiness to purify your Mind, let's play Cosmic Surrender ~
Need more Conviction! He knows there's a war to be thought!
No criticism to end Fascism, who'll die for the truth? Ask whom?
Blowing their minds with some Conceptual deconstructionism ~
I'll try a bit of that, breaking through 3rd dimensional barricades.
Who's stopping that raging beast rampaging in your street?
A threat to everything you accepted as True and beautiful ~
for your protection you've been given a New Nano Lobotomy

*

Out of Love
Rays shining brilliantly from your Violet Heart ~
They are the Masters of Maya in Maya in*finitum.
"You'll feel like a Sultan with 40 chicks sucking you!"
Or they're the SLAVES of their own creation; 'You're a King!'
Gone beyond ~ experiencing everything.
Now I want to be me

Delicious Lubriclity

She is gorgeous from behind ~ luscious in front.
Inhaling sweet perfumes, swooning with delight.
Lost her presence; You can possess her willingly.
"You may take up the position of prayer with your head
on the ground and your buttocks in the air"
Any posture you prefer ~ I like it All ways.
Let the revelation of the divine enter into me.
Keeping my promise to her ~ gliding in through her tight vulva,
soft touches and warm, hard thighs, languid eyes, nibbling her tits.
Clasping her tightly til she feels my Love, our passions blending!
Ready now for coition penetration* her pleasure will be supreme.
Animating, Livin' in the heat, being in Love with all the auras.
Finding someone to share it with ~ Sitting well with myself.
Standing in the Truth ~ It's making your heart sing

*

"Oh, Oh Oh Yeah ~ Oh God!"

Chain Reaction ~ Suddenly blasting out of gravity's trap on DMT.
'Your Mind has a Mind of its Own' ~ energy keeping you drugged.
Otherwise why have unwanted thoughts? Maya is still in Control.
Her life's made solely dependent on her husband; She is a Slave.
Will your Loving endure? Is this Virtue? Is this equal freedom?
'Rest your sword in her sheath' ~ don't waste a moment of bliss.
Draining the cup of pleasure, 'istening to her sighs and murmurs.
Keep grinding, pounding the Fruit, moist eyes, her signal to fuck ~
Explore her body fully, laying a provocative hand on her genitalia.
Sucking vagina, screaming copulation don't neglect any part of her.
Bring her to her favorite position ~ licking loaded cum from her lips.
Both Orgasming simultaneously is the greatest pleasure treasure.
"Let your mind be Free from all other thought"
Complete for both ~ the Secret of Love

Charmless Matrixcal Research

Mr. Vice President, Majestik's > One illegal criminal act a day!
Explaining all the exploding S4 Nukes out at Papoose Lake, NV.
Atomic Energy*make mine a Psychedelic Avatar in a Space*ship.
Taking a look at natural disasters ~ Soaked away in the Uranium.
The Cabals have lost their Nuclear Power bases, hip hip hooray!
Who OWNS our Air, Water, Energy, money, medicine, food etc?
Indoctrination of Information; Who is needing to Control Dissent?
Who's Controlling Y/our FREEDOM ~ Other's concepts of what?
Structure: Who needs to KNOW, who makes Secret decisions?
130,000 people working on the Unbeknown Manhattan Project!
Ominous All Seeing Eye ~ What's the Intentions of a dollar bill?
Addicted to your blood ~ change now to cool Unconditional Love.
I believe in the UFO's badge I wore as a kid.
It's a Tough decision letting go of the dream

*

Latent in us

'They believe he epitomizes the council house intellectual'
She had the best Telepathic capacity on the Planet; blew her up!
Nice to have hot Pleiadian girlfriends ~ 'We're just empty space'
She was trained to be Mother Goddess, collected by Red Cross.
They got best Sound Proofing in the bay for tortured Screaming.
Compart-mentalising all FEARS, Programming People's dreams.
We all got a John Wayne, heroic man in white Stetson Program.
Gave them a batch of DNA; brain, blood, Adrenalin, Endorphins.
That's not on many menus. A Church club for holiest Pedophiles.
Jesuit Junkies wanting it all! Better listen, this is sinisterly Real!
Gave us a wrong Model, spoken by a Doublespeak falling angel.
You have the right to Transform ~ so you can still live on Earth
being just You * Star seed becoming light * Zero matter energy!

Is there an Explanation?

*Need some strangeness, obtuse fish fingers floating in a dead
mercurial reef. This massive, aquatic collateral damage; WHY?
Turn the other eye, do you feel any urge to cry for those shrimp?
How about those shoals swallowed up in a plasticised lagoon or
stuck in an 'Illegal' net. Who set those parameters, quotas met!
Evoking Neptune for a fight back ~ mighty Poseidon's Trident
coming to a supermarket near you to upset the poison counter.
Taiji is on notice from the God of Dolphins for a revenge bout.
Unnatural Fukushima ~ there'll be no sushi left to shout about!
Who's exploiting nature's richness on an Industrial scale of greed?
This is not a virtual game of horrors; We need a change of heart*

*

Where Is Reality?

*'In the depths of sublime poetics ~ of Nietzsche and De Chirico'
'In mystery and melancholy, of shadows across a street at noon'
Scenes of Mannequins with vertigo falling into Surreal clarity.
Don't need any rational explications or any linear spirit levels.
Cut the fear from your eyes with light sharpened laser blades.
"Don't look back or you'll transmute into an Opium Poppy"
Open up the perceptions of your barricaded, razor wired minds.
Raze it to the ground and walk away with a smile on your face!
Can't slap them anymore have to use a tranquiliser gun, Taser!
Where did it come from? Does it really matter, accept it as it is!
'It's in your XX Paranormal stars* they'd lock you up in the UK!'
Given as an inspiring gift to suggest ~ Given as a visionary quest.
Flip it over, see from another tangent, multi dimensional dreams.
Wake up new and Marvelous, alive with each fantastic molecule.
Get a different perspective and reframe things; He Loves his drugs,
he loves his Valium, he Loves his hash, Loves his home made LSD.
Having a window pane into another Parallel Universe*

Embracing Nature's Ethers
We don't come together in the Collective ~ No Union, No Spirit!
Royal family's 'Public Relations Agency' - 'Rebranding Despots'
Don't respect FORM ... coming to do their drugs without Stress.
Fingers Crossed! "Ethics will topple Power" ~ 'Boom Bholenath'
Good Karma ~ still a Prisoner in a Cage of Diamonds... Fucked!
You have to get reborn*Siddhartha living in a Golden Penthouse!
R*evolution of stepping into the light ~ Giving with detachment.
"If we go into FEAR we have more SUFFERING"
Now 'Human Resources' for Happy Personnel!
*

Our Don's Destiny
One day working as a coolie at the docks when a crate broke open
and he found Gold biscuits ~ Enough biscuits to buy his own Mafia!
The new Sultan of the Underworld ~ but 'Lakshmi rules the World!'
Sacrifice your life for me and I'll look after your mum ~
Full Cash plus she got baksheesh in a bag of Jewels.
Kali Yuga Karma of desperate Greed ruling the Planet!
*

Who Is Ruling this Earth?
India's already been Nuked, their nervous system's still damaged ~
The Official recording of rape in India ~ is one every twenty minutes!
Girl chanting the Saraswati mantra, begging her attackers to Chelo!
Feudalists,"You can't just drill holes into a Sacred mountain!!!!"
"Wiping them out ~ tribals, poor farmers they get so poor they die!"
Allowing ourselves to see the Unseeable ~ gestural abstraction.
Innovazione* breaking the ancient codes of Cosmic frontiers.
Saw it from a distance, unique, original, creativity ~ poetry.
"The Silence around us is really the stillness within us"
Died from having too much pleasure*'Om Mani Padma Hum'
Stirring Your Love Vehicle

Who's Demonizing Whom?

A Recruitment agency servicing the brothels and Press Gangs.
Came the host of Black Death, Apocalyptic plague proportions!
Sunday 2nd September 1666, King's bakery, Pudding lane; Fire!
Massive bonfires blazed, full of smoke on all the street corners.
The wandering whores out catching sailors for a last sacrifice.
'Nuns and wives excluded ~ Protected from such Exploitation'.
'Satan's blessing East India Company for his King & Treasury'
Tying up their Dung boats to the wharves of Divine Retribution!
How can I trust you? Another sort of human matrix Controlling..
Who took away all Regulations crashing the World's Economy?
'They'll hang themselves with their own golden ropes of Greed.'
Their Selfish Idolatry

Shiny or Dull Entities

Light hits the Crystalline DNA. * producing the Hologram of us ~
An insect, carnivore, flower * brain mind endgame what's it all about?
Pachamama is filling that space with hormones, pheromones, organic
existence ~ Interacting with each instant. Does grass go to heaven?
Code written into every cell ~ changing, being evolution on a cusp.
Cosmic harmony ~ natural balance deep in the mushroom jungle.
We've earned the right to be here ~ it's the survival of the fittest!
Stepping out of human nature into Universal nature's mystery.
"When I was in the caravan in the morning and I heard
the corn rustling and I thought ~ what was that?"
He lost his cruise ship ~ ended up at Kali Valley
"Most people wouldn't dream of doing anything like that"
"Bayonet everybody!!!"" ~ Gotta ask Why?
"The last thing I want is to be a gangster"
"Perfect I'll give you a crystal right away"

Cosmic Vibrations

Mutual Attraction what could be better? 'Earth is a Free
Will Zone' who said? Tuning in to the Pleiadian Channel.
'Our Galaxy is 100 million light years across' "That's Big!"
Levels of density, gravity! '100 billion squared* stars.' A lot!
Taking you to higher levels of Consciousness ~ **Feel Space.**
Pull down the Razor Wire! Who's controlling Y/our Media?
Ask the rehabilitated Dalai Lama ~ about Public Affairs.
Humanity is a Design Experiment at the Frontier's edge.
The Planet is a Light Center of Information, ask your DNA.
It's the frequencies keeping them in or out of Power! Who?
Ask your reigning Plutocrat, Oligarch, Monarch, Sexy High Priestess.
They create all Emotional Traumas, keep feeding us our perceptions.
Crystal Nirvana soup! Needs original 12 strands not 2 strand energy.
Unplugged the Original * keeping us down in a quarantined dungeon.
Eyes of Horus connecting the whole hologram ~ Realising the Fear!
I want my free spirit uninhibited ~ multi*dimensionalities to fly high.
'Don't need to define things at all to raise a feeling'

*

Sitting on Dissociative Embroidered Cushions

The Non meaning of 'Uselessness' ~ Isn't there such a state?
'Met Man Ray at Place Saint Sulpice for my free self-portrait.'
Who needs practical dreamers to create ~ Mosaics, collages,
Lindisfarne Illuminated manuscripts and Mughal Kama sutras?
Depictions of illicit entrances & exits for young men entering the
harem when the King is absent from the Palace on a pilgrimage.
Let's have a shag with the most preciously desirable courtesans.
Don't let any beautiful innocent girl be corrupted by wickedness.
All things are connected by Love, act on your own best inclination.
Affection awakening the radiant sucker ~ introducing your cock!
It's difficult living up to the expectations of someone who is in Love.

2b 2gether in * time ~ Space

"I was sitting in Chapora at three in the morning ~ Shaking!"
Not easy to find normal in Goa ~ Peacocks dancing in your garden!
"Rather than worry about it let it happen" ~ Move on, move on, move.
Fitting into the environment we're all together ~ Sane in our Asylum.
We're Not all mad, 'those well adjusted to their sick society are mad'
Feeling Psychedelic*Cosmic energy, platinum blue rays ~ resonating.
Opening up to Sacred geometry ~ with trippy Shakti; IT IS the Real.
Look into her eyes and see there's no boundaries ~ becoming One.
Beautiful Magic * Tantric mysteries, easy to do ~ in a stream of light

*

No Time ~ Frequency

So filled, no times to waste ~ in that, relaxed at the speed of light.
Don't let the Mind take over with the 'Thought' ~ Don't fester on it!
It might put all sorts of ideas in your head. 'A Peacock's open Fan!'
Simply, Symmetry *Be ~ Accept its Absolute transcendental nature.
Honestly, there's nothing to hold onto ~ It is Impossible!
Respect for the people dealing with Cosmic Love Conscious.
Let it go until it burns itself up ~ Offering of Magical Protection

*

Accidentally On Purpose

CELEBRATE the *ACT* of LIFE!
"Come and Feast!" ~ A trip to God!
"I'm a busy guy ~ dancing in ecstasy!"
Amazing Clarity, opening the all seeing eye
"Pulling the Sun * light ~ Love into me & sending it out to everyone"
Conducive, creative reflections, smooth Inside ~ in your Shakti eyes.
"I must go and dance for the HAPPINESS of All People"
It will be what it will be ~ Wholeness, it's in the happening.
It already is in the waters ~ accept it ~ Unity of fe/male
The Primary Mandala transmuting it all.
Use All The Rainbow

ABOUT SUNNY JETSUN

*Inspired by the sixties Sunny started traveling the world in 1970.
His spiritual journey on the hippie trail to India took him through
San Francisco, Los Angeles, London, Amsterdam, Paris, Vancouver,
Sidney and Kathmandu to Varanasi. His arrival on the sub-continent
was the beginning of writing autobiographical verses capturing his travel
experiences, encounters with remarkable people and his quest for self-
realization. Combining experimentation with drugs, sex, rock & roll ~
meditation, Love and life in general. Sunny started to open up to a multi-
dimensional Universe. He lived the mantra, "Turn on, tune in, drop out"
realising Mind's-illusions, inspired by deeper feelings of holistic nature,
empathy*energy & Space.*

*Over four decades Sunny has written and published 28 books of poetry,
created over one hundred paintings, traveled the World and considers
his masterpiece to be his daughter. He has spent the past fifteen years
in Goa, India inspired by the freedom to experience and idealism of
human consciousness.*

Sunny Jetsun books and art are available on the web at:

*Website: www.sunnyjetsun.com
Facebook: www.facebook.com/sunnyjetsun
Amazon: www.amazon.com/author/sunnyjetsun
Smashwords: www.smashwords.com/profile/view/sunnyjetsun*

www.ingramcontent.com/pod-product-compliance
Lightning Source LLC
Chambersburg PA
CBHW020508030426
42337CB00011B/290